BERRIED TREASURES

COOKBOOK

JUST POSSIBLY THE MOST
SCRUMPTIOUS COLLECTION OF
BERRY RECIPES EVER ASSEMBLED

by: ELAINE JAUMAN

THIS COOKBOOK IS

DEDICATED TO GOOD COOKS,

AND BERRY LOVERS EVERYWHERE!

Copyright 1982 by Elaine Jauman
1st printing, June 1982, 2,000 copies
2nd printing, July 1982, 2,000 copies

Revised Edition
1st printing, April 1983, 5,000 copies

Published by
KITCHEN TREASURES
810 First Avenue South
Escanaba, Michigan 49829

Cover and Illustrations by
PHOTO OFFSET PRINTING
Escanaba, Michigan

ISBN 0-9609282-3-5

We all have our favorite or "treasured" berry. It's no wonder that berry picking is a much enjoyed past time of many people, but "Berried treasures" are not only acquired by people, but also by bears, deer, birds, and other forest dwellers. If you have ever eaten a handful of freshly picked berries, you can understand why they are so highly treasured by people as well as animals!

"Berried treasures" can be found on any national forest land, and no permit is required to pick these berries. The only requirement is that they be gathered for personal use only. It is extremely important that you be able to recognize and identify the berries picked. Not all berries are edible--some are merely distasteful, others are poisonous. A good rule to follow is that unless you are absolutely sure of which kind of berry it is, better leave it on the bush.

Of course, there are many commercial berry farms that offer your choice "treasure." If you want strawberries, raspberries, or blueberries, you can pick as many as your heart desires for a reasonable price, usually per pound.

BERRIED TREASURES COOKBOOK is the ultimate result of one of America's favorite past times. I hope you will enjoy making and eating the many scrumptious recipes in this cookbook as much as I have enjoyed compiling them for you!

Additional copies of Berried Treasures or More Berried Treasures and Other Good Pickin's may be ordered by sending your name, address and $4.95 plus $1.00 postage and handling for each book ordered OR $10.50 postpaid for any two cookbooks to:

KITCHEN TREASURES

P.O. Box 541
Osseo, MN 55369

ACKNOWLEDGMENTS

A "berry" special thank you to the following companies:

BORDEN, INC.

CALIFORNIA APRICOT ADVISORY BOARD

COCORIBE COMPANY

DURKEE FAMOUS FOODS

H. J. HEINZ COMPANY

KELLOGG'S

KNOX GELATINE

LEROUX IMPORTED LIQUEURS

LOUIS SHERRY ICE CREAM COMPANY

OSTER

SWIFT & COMPANY

and individuals:

Shelly Oja

Dorothy Srock

Judy Tulgren

and numerous relatives and friends

whose cooperation and expertise helped make this cookbook possible.

Also, last but certainly not least, thank you to my husband and four children who helped create, eat, and bear with me through the making of BERRIED TREASURES!

* * *

TABLE OF CONTENTS

DEFINITIONS

BAVARIAN CREAM - a soufflelike dessert made with custard, gelatin and whipped cream as in "Strawberries Bavarian."

BOMBE - a round or melon-shaped frozen mold made from a combination of ice creams, mousses, or ices as in "Brandied Raspberry Bombe."

CHANTILLY - (of food) prepared or served with whipped cream as in "Strawberries Chantilly."

CHIFFON - (in cooking) having a light, frothy texture, as certain pies and cakes containing beaten egg whites as in "Strawberry Chiffon Pie."

FLUMMERY - a type of fruit custard usually thickened with cornstarch as in "Bilberry Flummery."

FOOL - British Cookery - a dish made of fruit, scalded or stewed, crushed and mixed with cream or the like as in "Gooseberry Fool."

MELBA SAUCE - a clear raspberry sauce used esp. as a dessert topping as in "Peaches Melba."

MOUSSE - a sweetened preparation with whipped cream as a base, often stabilized with gelatin and chilled in a mold as in "Strawberry-Chocolate Mousse."

PARFAIT - 1)a dessert made of layers of ice cream and fruit, syrup, etc. usually topped with whipped cream. 2)a rich, frozen dessert of whipped cream and egg, variously flavored as in "Strawberry Parfait Pie" or "Cloud-Topped Parfait."

TORTE - a rich cake, esp. one containing little or no flour, usually made with eggs, crumbs and ground nuts as in "Blueberry Torte" or "Elegant Strawberry Torte."

TRIFLE - English Cookery - a dessert consisting of custard or some substitute and usually containing cake soaked in wine or liqueur, and jam, fruit or the like as in "Raspberry Trifle I or II."

* * *

BLUEBERRIES

FRESH BLUEBERRY PIE I

4 c. fresh blueberries   Dash of salt
1 c. sugar   1 Tbl. butter or margarine
4 Tbls. flour   Pastry for 2 crust 10-
                                  inch pie

Gently mix blueberries, sugar, flour and salt and turn
into pastry-lined pie plate. Dot with butter and top with
top crust. Slit top to allow steam to escape. Bake at
450° for 20 to 30 minutes or until crust is nicely brown.
Serve warm with ice cream or cold with whipped cream.

* * *

FRESH BLUEBERRY PIE II

4 c. blueberries, washed   4 Tbls. tapioca
  and drained   1 egg
½ c. granulated sugar   Pastry for 2 crust 9-
½ c. packed brown sugar   inch pie

Mix sugars, tapioca and egg. Stir in berries. Place in
bottom crust and top with lattice pattern. Bake at 400°
for 45 minutes or until crust is nicely brown.

* * *

FRESH BLUEBERRY PIE III

Pastry for 2 crust 8-in. pie   3 Tbls. cornstarch
3 c. fresh blueberries   2 Tbls. lemon juice
2/3 c. sugar   1½ Tbls. margarine

Mix dry ingredients lightly with blueberries. Sprinkle
with lemon juice. Put filling into pastry-lined pan.
Dot with margarine. Top with second crust and slit to
allow steam to escape. Bake at 400° for 50 minutes to
1 hour, or until filling bubbles and crust is golden.

* * *

EASY BLUEBERRY/CHEESE PIE

1 9-in. baked pie shell   3/4 tsp vanilla
1 (3 oz.) pkg. cream cheese   1 c. whipping cream
½ c. confectioners' sugar   2 c. blueberry pie filling

Mix cream cheese, sugar and vanilla. Whip the cream and
add to cheese mixture. Pour into pie shell. Cover top
of pie with blueberry pie filling. Chill overnight.

* * *

BLUEBERRY COMPOTE

Wash and drain 1 cup fresh blueberries. Sprinkle with
2 tablespoons sugar and fold carefully into 1 cup plain
yogurt!

* * *

7

BLUEBERRY DELIGHT PIE

1 9-in. graham cracker crust
1 envelope whipped topping
   dessert mix
1 (8 oz.) pkg. cream cheese,
   softened

$\frac{1}{4}$ c. confectioners' sugar
$\frac{1}{4}$ tsp. vanilla
$\frac{1}{2}$ c. chopped pecans
1 c. canned blueberry
   pie filling

Prepare whipped dessert topping according to package directions. Beat in cream cheese, sugar and vanilla until smooth. Stir in nuts. Pour into graham cracker crust. Top with pie filling. Chill at least 3 hours.

* * *

ARCTIC BLUEBERRY PIE

1 (5 oz.) pkg. pretzel sticks
$\frac{1}{2}$ c. butter or margarine,
   softened
1 quart vanilla ice cream

1 (21 oz.) can blueberry
   pie filling
1 tsp. almond extract

Crush pretzels to make $1\frac{1}{2}$ cups coarse crumbs. Place in a 9-inch pie plate; add butter and mix well. Press into bottom and sides of pan and refrigerate about 1 hour. Soften ice cream slightly and spoon into pretzel shell; wrap and freeze. Just before serving, combine blueberry pie filling and almond extract. Spoon filling into center of pie and let stand about 5 minutes; cut and serve.

* * *

BLUEBERRY CREAM CHEESE PIE

$1\frac{1}{2}$ c. fresh blueberries,
   rinsed and drained
1 (8 oz.) pkg. and 1 (3 oz.)
   pkg. cream cheese, softened
1 Tbl. flour

3 eggs, separated
$\frac{1}{4}$ c. sugar
$\frac{1}{2}$ tsp. salt
3/4 c. sour cream
Unbaked 9-inch pie shell

Using fork, stir softened cream cheese until smooth. Mix in flour. Beat egg whites until stiff, gradually adding sugar. Beat yolks and add salt and sour cream. Combine egg mixtures with cream cheese mixture, stirring well. Place drained blueberries on bottom of unbaked pie shell. Smooth cream cheese and egg mixture evenly over blueberries and bake in preheated moderate oven (350°F.) for 45 minutes or until set.

* * *

MINTED BLUEBERRIES

Combine a little orange juice with some chopped mint leaves; pour over fresh or dry-packed frozen blueberries. Sprinkle with confectioners' sugar. Chill. Just before serving, place in individual serving dishes and garnish with a mint leaf, if desired.

* * *

BLUEBERRY ALMOND PIE

1 qt. fresh blueberries,   1 Tbl. butter or margarine
   rinsed and drained   1 Tbl. Courvoisier,
3/4 c. sugar   (optional)
½ c. water   ¼ c. slivered almonds
2 Tbls. cornstarch dissolved   1 9-in. baked pie shell
   in 2 Tbls. water   Vanilla ice cream

In saucepan, combine 1 cup blueberries, sugar and water.
Bring slowly to a boil. Cook 10 minutes or until berries
are soft. Cool 5 minutes. Pureé in blender or food processor or rub mixture through sieve. Return to saucepan;
add cornstarch. Cook lightly over moderate heat until
mixture is thick. Stir in butter and Courvoisier; cool
slightly. Add slivered almonds. Combine with remaining
blueberries, reserving ½ cup berries for garnish. Mix
gently. Spoon into pie shell and refrigerate for several
hours. Just before serving, garnish with vanilla ice cream
and reserved blueberries.

* * *

TRIPLE LAYERED BLUEBERRY PIE

1 (16 oz.) can blueberries   ½ tsp. vanilla
1 (8 3/4 oz.) can crushed   1 9-in. baked pie shell
   pineapple   ¼ c. sugar
1 (8 oz.) pkg. cream cheese,   2 Tbls. cornstarch
   softened   ¼ tsp. salt
3 Tbls. sugar   1 tsp. lemon juice
1 Tbl. milk   ½ c. heavy cream, whipped

Drain fruits; reserve syrups. Blend cream cheese and next
3 ingredients. Reserve 2 tablespoons pineapple; stir remainder into cheese mixture. Spread over bottom of cooled
pie shell; chill. Blend ¼ cup sugar, cornstarch and salt.
Combine reserved syrups; measure 1½ cups; blend into cornstarch mixture. Cook and stir until thickened. Stir in
blueberries and lemon juice; cool. Pour over cheese layer;
chill. Before serving, top with whipped cream and reserved
pineapple.

* * *

BLUEBERRY SPONGE-TOPPED PUDDING

1 can (21 oz.) blueberry   ½ c. all-purpose flour
   pie filling   1 tsp. vanilla extract
2 eggs, beaten   1 tsp. baking powder
1 c. sugar   Plain or whipped cream

Put filling in an 8-inch square pan. Mix reamining ingredients thoroughly, except cream, and pour over blueberry
filling. Bake in 350° oven for 35 minutes. Serve warm
with cream. Serves 6.

* * *

BLUEBERRY PUMPKIN RUM PIE

3 eggs, separated
½ c. sugar
1½ c. cooked mashed pumpkin
½ c. milk
½ tsp. salt
½ tsp. each cinnamon,
   ginger, and nutmeg
2 tsp. rum flavoring

¼ tsp. Angostura aromatic
   bitters
1 envelope unflavored
   gelatin
¼ c. cold water
½ c. sugar
2 c. fresh blueberries,
   washed and drained
1 baked 9-in. pie shell

In a saucepan, combine egg yolks, sugar, pumpkin, milk, salt and spices. Stir over low heat until mixture thickens. Mix together rum flavoring, bitters, gelatin and water. Stir mixture into hot pumpkin mixture until gelatin is dissolved. Chill until cold and slightly thickened. Beat egg whites until stiff. Gradually beat in sugar, 1 tablespoon at a time, until glossy. Fold egg whites and blueberries into pumpkin mixture. Pour mixture into baked pie shell. Chill until firm. Serve with the following topping:

TOPPING: Combine 1 cup whipping cream, whipped, 1 cup fresh blueberries and 1 tablespoon rum flavoring.

* * *

BLUEBERRY PIE SUPREME

1 9-in. unbaked pie shell
1 (21 oz.) can blueberry
   pie filling
4 (3 oz.) pkg. cream cheese,
   softened

½ c. sugar
2 eggs
½ tsp. vanilla
1 c. dairy sour cream

Spread half of blueberry pie filling in bottom of unbaked pie crust and bake at 425°F. for 15 minutes or until crust is golden brown. Reduce oven temperature to 350°F. Beat cream cheese, sugar, eggs and vanilla until smooth. Pour over hot blueberry filling and bake 25 minutes. (Filling will be slightly soft in center). Cool. Before serving, spoon sour cream around edge of pie and fill center with remaining blueberry pie filling.

* * *

BLUEBERRY AMBROSIA

1 lg. pkg. vanilla pudding mix
2 c. fresh blueberries,
   washed and drained

2 lg. oranges, peeled
   and sectioned
½ c. shredded coconut

Cook pudding according to package directions; cool. In deep dessert dishes, pour a layer of chilled pudding, a layer of sliced oranges, and a layer of fresh blueberries. Sprinkle top with coconut. Repeat 5 more times. Makes 6 servings.

* * *

MICHIGAN COMPOTE

6 lg. Michigan peaches, sliced   Dash of ginger
1 pint Michigan blueberries   Dash of nutmeg (optional)
1 Tbl. lemon juice   1 pint sour cream OR
1/3 c. sugar   whipping cream

Sprinkle lemon juice over peaches. Add sugar and blueberries and mix lightly. Let stand until sugar is dissolved.
Spoon into dishes and top with sour cream or whipped cream
to which you have added the ginger and nutmeg, if desired.

* * *

BLUEBERRY WATERMELON SALAD

1 c. blueberries   2 Tbls. lime juice
1 c. honeydew melon chunks $\frac{1}{2}$ c. dairy sour cream
2 c. watermelon balls   4 lettuce cups
3 Tbls. honey

Combine fruits in deep bowl. Combine honey and lime juice;
pour over fruit. Cover with foil or clear plastic wrap
and marinate 2 to 3 hours in refrigerator, stirring several
times to distribute sauce evenly. Drain fruits, reserving
2 tablespoons liquid. Combine dairy sour cream and the
reserved liquid, stirring to blend. Pile fruits into lettuce cups. Top with sour cream dressing. Serve immediately. Makes 4 servings.

* * *

FRUIT 'N CHICKEN MOLD

2 envelopes unflavored gelatin   1 c. apple juice
$2\frac{1}{2}$ c. orange juice   1 c. chicken, cut in chunks
$\frac{1}{2}$ tsp. cinnamon   1 c. blueberries
Dash of ground cloves   1 c. peaches, diced

In a saucepan, sprinkle gelatin over orange juice to soften
and add cinnamon and cloves. Bring to a boil, stirring
until gelatin is dissolved. Remove from heat and add apple
juice. Chill until slightly thickened. Fold in remaining
ingredients and pour into a 6-cup mold. Chill until firm.
Makes 4 servings.

* * *

BLUEBERRY-PINEAPPLE SALAD

1 lg. pkg. lime gelatin   1 c. fresh blueberries,
2 c. boiling water   rinsed and drained
1 can crushed pineapple   1 c. dairy sour cream

Dissolve gelatin in boiling water. Add pineapple and syrup
and chill until thickened. Add blueberries and sour cream,
mixing gently. Pour into a $1\frac{1}{2}$-quart mold and chill until
set.

* * *

MINTED BLUEBERRY FREEZE

2/3 c. mint flavored
  apple jelly
1 c. salad dressing
1 c. miniature marshmallows

1 c. diced pears
1 1/3 c. fresh blueberries
1 c. whipping cream,
  whipped

Melt jelly over low heat; gradually add to salad dressing, mixing well. Add marshmallows and fruit; fold in whipped cream. Pour into a 1½-quart mold; freeze. Unmold and garnish with additional salad dressing. Makes 6 to 8 servings.

* * *

FRUIT-RICE SALAD

To leftover cooked rice, add seedless green or halved pitted grapes, diced peeled orange, pineapple chunks and blueberries. Combine mayonnaise with a little lemon juice and fold into fruit/rice combination.

* * *

FRUIT SALAD COMBINATION

Lightly mix 2 cups cantaloupe cubes; ½ cup fresh blueberries; and 1 large banana, sliced. Serve on crisp salad greens allowing about ½ cup per serving.

* * *

BLUEBERRY RAINBOW MELON

Scoop out cantaloupe halves with melon ball cutter. Fill shells with fresh blueberries and melon balls. Top with generous scoops of rainbow sherbet.

A refreshing summer dessert!

* * *

BLUEBERRY OATMEAL BREAD

2 c. flour
1 tsp. baking powder
1 tsp. baking soda
1 tsp. salt
½ tsp. nutmeg
1 c. quick-cooking oats

1/3 c. soft shortening
½ c. packed brown sugar
2 eggs
1 c. sour milk or buttermilk
1 c. chopped pecans
1½ c. fresh blueberries

Preheat oven to 350°F. and generously grease a 9x5x3-inch loaf pan. In a large bowl combine flour, baking powder, soda, salt and nutmeg. Stir in oats. In a small bowl, beat shortening, brown sugar and eggs until fluffy. Slowly beat in buttermilk. Make a well in the center of flour mixture and pour in egg mixture; stirring with a fork just until dry ingredients are moistened and well blended. Gently fold in nuts and well-drained blueberries. Pour into pan and bake 60 minutes or until cake tests done.

* * *

BLUEBERRY ORANGE BREAD I

2 Tbls. margarine	1 c. sugar
¼ c. boiling water	2 c. all-purpose flour
2/3 c. orange juice	½ tsp. salt
4 tsp. grated orange rind	¼ tsp. soda
1 c. fresh blueberries	1 tsp. baking powder
1 egg	2 Tbls. honey

Melt margarine in boiling water in small bowl. Add ½ cup orange juice and 3 teaspoons rind. Beat egg and sugar until light and fluffy. Combine dry ingredients and add alternately with orange liquid, beating until smooth. Fold in blueberries. Bake in greased 1½-quart ring baking dish. Turn out onto plate. Mix 2 tablespoons orange juice and 1 teaspoon rind and 2 tablespoons honey; spoon over hot loaf.

* * *

BLUEBERRY ORANGE BREAD II

2 c. all-purpose flour	½ c. chopped walnuts
½ c. sugar	1 tsp. grated orange
1½ tsp. baking powder	peel
½ tsp. salt	1 egg
½ tsp. baking soda	3/4 c. orange juice
1 c. blueberries	2 Tbls. oil

Sprinkle blueberries with a bit of flour and toss lightly. Combine flour, sugar, baking powder, salt and baking soda. Stir in blueberries, nuts, and orange peel. Set aside. Combine egg, orange juice and salad oil. Add to flour/fruit mixture. Stir just until moistened. Pour into greased and floured 9x5-inch loaf pan. Bake at 350°F. for 50 minutes or until lightly browned.

* * *

EASY BLUEBERRY SKILLET BREAD

1 pkg. (13½ oz.) blueberry	2/3 c. milk
muffin mix	3 Tbls. butter or
1 egg	margarine

Prepare blueberry muffin mix using 1 egg and 2/3 cup milk, mixing until fairly smooth. Heat 2 tablespoons butter in a 10-inch skillet and pour in batter. Cover and cook over low heat 10 minutes, or until browned around edges and set. Turn over onto cookie sheet. Put remaining tablespoon butter in skillet; when melted, slip bread back into skillet. Continue cooking over low heat 5 minutes, or until done.

* * *

MICHIGAN BLUEBERRY PUDDING

1½ c. fresh Michigan
   blueberries
2½ c. all-purpose flour
¼ c. butter, softened
3/4 c. Michigan sugar

1 egg, well beaten
½ tsp. vanilla extract
½ tsp. lemon extract
½ tsp. baking soda
1 c. buttermilk

Grease 1-quart pudding mold thoroughly, including inside of the cover (or use coffee can and cover top with heavy-duty aluminum foil). Pick over blueberries and wash well; dry on absorbent paper. When dry, toss lightly with about 1 tablespoon of the flour. Cream butter and sugar together until light and fluffy. Beat in egg; stir in vanilla and lemon extracts. Combine baking soda with buttermilk, stirring well. Add flour and buttermilk alternately to creamed butter, beginning and ending with flour; blend thoroughly. Fold in floured blueberries. Turn into mold and smooth out top. Cover securely with lid (or tie foil over top of coffee can). Place on a rack in a large pot. Pour in sufficient boiling water to come within 1 inch of top of mold. Cover pot tightly, bring to a boil, reduce heat, and steam 3 hours, adding more boiling water during cooking period as needed. Lift mold carefully from the pot. Remove lid and run a knife around edge of pudding. Turn out on serving platter and serve warm with hard sauce or whipped cream. Makes 6 to 8 servings.

* * *

BLUEBERRY BUCKLE

1½ c. fresh blueberries
¼ c. flour
¼ c. sugar
1 c. sour cream
1 tsp. vanilla
2 eggs

3/4 c. flour
½ c. brown sugar
½ c. coconut
¼ tsp. cinnamon
¼ c. softened margarine

Place washed and drained blueberries on bottom of ungreased 8-inch square pan. Combine ¼ cup flour, ¼ cup sugar, sour cream, vanilla and eggs; beat until smooth. Pour over berries. Combine remaining ingredients and sprinkle over sour cream mixture. Bake 350°F. for 30 to 40 minutes or until puffed and brown. Serve warm or cold.

* * *

Blueberries are nature's original convenience food. You don't have to pit, peel or hull them...simply wash and enjoy by the handful!

* * *

BLUEBERRY YEAST CAKE

1 c. milk
¼ c. granulated sugar
1 tsp. salt
¼ c. butter or margarine
½ c. warm water

1 pkg. active dry yeast
4 eggs
5 c. flour
1 c. fresh blueberries,
   washed and drained

In a small saucepan, heat milk just until it begins to bubble around the edges. Remove from heat and add sugar, salt and butter, stirring until butter is melted. Cool to lukewarm. Sprinkle yeast over warm water in a large bowl, stirring to dissolve. Add milk mixture, eggs and 4 cups flour. Beat until smooth. Add remaining flour, beating with a spoon until batter is smooth. Cover bowl with waxed paper and damp towel and let rise in warm place to within 1 inch of top of bowl (about 1 hour). Grease a 10-inch tube pan. Beat batter hard for about 30 seconds and fold in blueberries. Turn batter into tube pan and let rise to within 1 inch of top of pan (about 1 hour). Preheat oven to 350°F. and bake 45 to 50 minutes or until golden brown. Turn out onto wire rack and cool partially.

Top with confectioners' sugar glaze made with 1 cup confectioners' sugar and 1 tablespoon milk. Serve warm.

* * *

BLUEBERRY REFRIGERATOR CAKE

1 c. sugar
2 tsp. cinnamon
2 Tbls. water

1 quart blueberries
10 slices bread, approx.
3 Tbls. butter

Wash and drain blueberries. Mix cinnamon and sugar and add to blueberries. Add water. Bring to boil and set aside. Spread butter on bread, then cut in strips. Line bottom of a bread pan with the bread strips. Pour about 1/3 of the blueberries over bread. Add another layer of bread and continue layering, ending with a layer of bread. Chill overnight.

* * *

BLUEBERRY PIE FILLING CAKE

1 c. oil
2 c. sugar
4 eggs
3 tsp. vanilla
4 c. flour
4 tsp. baking soda

½ tsp. salt
½ c. orange juice
1 (21 oz.) can blueberry
   pie filling
Cinnamon
Sugar

Cream oil with sugar, eggs and vanilla. Combine dry ingredients and add alternately with orange juice to creamed mixture. Put 3/4 of the batter in bottom of greased 10x14-inch pan. Put blueberries on top; pour remaining batter over all. Sprinkle with cinnamon and sugar. Bake at 350° for 1 hour.

15

BLUEBERRY CAKE TOPPED WITH VANILLA SAUCE

2/3 c. sugar
1 egg
1½ c. cake flour, sifted
2 tsp. baking powder
½ tsp. salt
1/3 c. milk

3 Tbls. butter or
    margarine, melted
1 tsp. vanilla extract
1 c. fresh blueberries,
    washed and drained
Vanilla sauce*

Gradually add sugar to egg, beating until blended. Add dry ingredients alternately with milk to first mixture, beating until smooth. Stir in butter and vanilla. Fold in blueberries and pour into greased 9x5-inch loaf pan. Bake at 400°F. for 30 minutes or until cake tests done. Turn out of pan and serve warm with vanilla sauce.

*VANILLA SAUCE: Combine 1 cup sugar and 2 tablespoons cornstarch in a small saucepan. Stir in 2 cups boiling water and cook, stirring until thickened. Stir in ¼ cup butter or margarine, 2 teaspoons vanilla and a dash of nutmeg. Serve warm.

* * *

DELICATE BLUEBERRY CAKE

2 c. all-purpose flour
1 c. granulated sugar
2 tsp. baking powder
1 tsp. cinnamon
½ tsp. nutmeg

½ c. butter or
    margarine, softened
2 eggs
1 (10 oz.) pkg. frozen
    blueberries, thawed

Preheat oven to 350°F. Grease and lightly flour a 9-inch square baking pan. In large bowl, sift together first 5 ingredients. With electric mixer at low speed, beat in butter until mixture resembles coarse crumbs. Add eggs and 3/4 cup water; beat 1 minute or until blended. Spread batter evenly in pan; sprinkle drained blueberries evenly over top. Bake 1 hour or until golden brown. Serve hot or cold.

* * *

CENTURY OLD BLUEBERRY CAKE

1/3 tsp. salt
2/3 c. plus 1 Tbl. sugar
1/3 c. butter
1 2/3 c. flour

1 egg
1/3 c. milk
1½ tsp. baking powder
1 c. fresh blueberries

Cream sugar and butter together and add egg; mix until light in color. Sift flour, salt and baking powder together. Add dry ingredients alternately with milk to first mixture. Fold in blueberries and bake at 375°F. for 30 minutes in a 9-inch lightly greased pan.

* * *

16

BLUEBERRY LAST MINUTE TORTE

1 purchased sponge cake
1 c. whipping cream, whipped
1 c. sour cream
1 (13 oz.) can crushed
   pineapple, drained
1 Tbl. mayonnaise

1 c. fresh blueberries,
   rinsed and drained
½ c. graham cracker crumbs
¼ c. granulated sugar
½ tsp. cinnamon

Divide cake into 3 layers. Mix next 5 ingredients. Layer and frost. Decorate sides with crumbs, sugar and cinnamon mixture. Chill.

* * *

EASY BLUEBERRY POUNDCAKE

1 pkg. pound cake mix
1 c. fresh blueberries
1/3 c. chopped nuts
1/3 c. raisins

½ tsp. cinnamon
½ tsp. nutmeg
2 c. confectioners' sugar
Lemon juice

Prepare pound cake according to package directions. When batter is ready, gently fold in blueberries, nuts, raisins, and spices. Pour mixture into 3 greased and floured 5½x3-inch loaf pans. Bake according to package directions, allowing 10 minutes less baking time. Unmold and cool on rack. Mix confectioners' sugar with enough lemon juice to make a glaze the consistency of heavy cream. Spread on cooled poundcake. Do not slice before thoroughly cool.

* * *

BLUEBERRY UPSIDE-DOWN CAKE

2 c. fresh blueberries
3/4 c. sugar
2 Tbls. flour
2 Tbls. lemon juice
   ***
½ c. shortening
1 c. sugar
3 eggs

2 c. all-purpose flour
3 tsp. baking powder
1 tsp. salt
3/4 c. milk
1½ c. coarsely chopped
   nutmeats
Grated rind of 1 orange
Confectioners' sugar

Combine blueberries with next 3 ingredients. Spread mixture in reased 8x12-inch baking pan. Cream shortening and gradually beat in sugar. Beat in eggs one at a time. Sift flour, baking powder and salt. Alternately add dry ingredients and milk, beginning and ending with the dry ingredients. Fold in nuts and orange rind. Pour batter over blueberries. Bake in preheated oven 350°F. for 45 minutes or until cake feels firm to touch. Invert while still hot; serve warm, sprinkled with confectioners' sugar.

* * *

BLUEBERRY TEA LOAVES

1 pkg. pound cake mix
1 c. fresh blueberries,
   rinsed and drained, OR
   1 can (15 oz.) blue-
   berries, drained

1/3 c. chopped nuts
1/3 c. raisins
$\frac{1}{2}$ tsp. ground cinnamon
$\frac{1}{2}$ tsp. ground nutmeg
2 c. confectioners' sugar
   Lemon juice

Prepare pound cake mix according to package directions. When batter is ready, gently fold in blueberries, nuts, raisins and spices. Pour mixture into 3 greased and floured 3x5$\frac{1}{2}$x2-inch loaf pans. (If small pans are not available, use two regular-size pans.) Bake according to package directions allowing 10 minutes less baking time. Unmold and cool on a rack. Mix confectioners' sugar with enough lemon juice until the consistency of heavy cream. Spoon glaze over loaves. Cool thoroughly before slicing.

* * *

BLUEBERRY CAKE

To any of your favorite cake mix batters, carefully fold in 2 cups washed and dried blueberries for a 2-layer cake. Bake in layer-cake pans or in square or rectangular pans. (Or you can use 2 cans (15 oz. ea.) blueberries, well drained and rinsed. Fold in gently to prevent crushing berries.)

* * *

BLUEBERRY STREUSEL CAKE

1 pkg. (14$\frac{1}{2}$ oz.) cinnamon streusel coffee cake mix
2 cups fresh blueberries, rinsed and drained

Prepare coffee cake batter according to directions on package. Pour batter into a well-greased 9-inch square or round pan. Sprinkle blueberries over the top of the batter. Sprinkle streusel topping over the top of the blueberries. Bake in a moderate oven (375°) for 35 to 40 minutes or until top is deep brown. Cool cake in pan and cut into squares or wedges while still warm. Serve warm. Yield: 1 9-inch round or square.

* * *

18

BLUEBERRY MUFFINS

1 egg
1 c. milk
1/3 c. oil or melted
   shortening
2 c. flour

1 Tbl. baking powder
1 tsp. salt
½ c. sugar
3/4 c. fresh blueberries,
   washed and drained

Beat egg until yolk and white are well blended. Blend
in milk and oil. Mix dry ingredients thoroughly. Add
liquid and stir until dry ingredients are barely moistened.
Do not overmix. Batter should be lumpy. Lightly blend
in blueberries. Do not crush berries. Fill greased or
paper-lined muffin tins half full of batter. Bake at
400° for 20 to 25 minutes.

* * *

BLUEBERRY OATMEAL MUFFINS

3 c. biscuit mix
½ c. firmly packed dark brown
   sugar
3/4 c. quick-cooking oats
1 tsp. ground cinnamon

2 eggs, well beaten
1½ c. milk
¼ c. butter or margarine,
   melted
2 c. fresh blueberries

Rinse and drain blueberries. Combine biscuit mix, brown
sugar, oatmeal and cinnamon. Mix eggs, milk and butter.
Add to dry ingredients all at once and stir until just
blended. Fold in blueberries. Spoon into greased muffin
pans, filling cups 2/3 full. Bake in a preheated hot
oven (400°) for 15 to 20 minutes or until golden brown.
Remove from pan and cool on a rack. Makes 18 muffins.

* * *

BLUEBERRY HONEY MUFFINS

6 Tbls. butter or margarine
3/4 c. honey
2 eggs
2 c. whole wheat flour

4 tsp. baking powder
½ c. milk
2 tsp. cinnamon
2 c. fresh blueberries

Rinse and drain blueberries. Cream butter or margarine
and honey; add eggs and beat well. Combine dry ingredients
and add to batter alternately with milk. Crush ½ cup
blueberries and add to batter by hand, then fold in rest
of blueberries. Grease bottom of muffin tins and fill
very full. Bake at 375° for 25 to 30 minutes or until
nicely brown. Cool before removing from pan. Makes 12
muffins.

* * *

BLUEBERRY SHORTCAKE MUFFINS

2 c. biscuit mix
¼ c. sugar
½ tsp. cinnamon
1 c. sour cream

1 egg
1 c. fresh blueberries,
  rinsed and drained
6 tsp. granulated sugar

Preheat oven to 425°. In a medium bowl combine biscuit mix, ¼ cup sugar and cinnamon, mixing well. Make a well in center of mixture and add sour cream all at once, then egg; beat with a fork until well combined. Gently fold in blueberries and fill paper-lined muffin cups about half full. Sprinkle top of each with ½ teaspoon sugar. Bake about 20 minutes, or until nicely brown. Serve hot. Makes 12 muffins.

* * *

BLUEBERRY CAKE MUFFINS

2 c. flour
1½ tsp. baking powder
¼ tsp. salt
½ c. butter or margarine,
  softened
1 c. fresh blueberries

1 c. sugar
2 eggs
1 tsp. vanilla extract
½ c. milk
Confectioners' sugar

Beat butter or margarine, sugar, eggs and vanilla until light and fluffy. Combine flour, baking powder and salt and add alternately with milk, beginning and ending with flour mixture. Beat just until smooth. Gently fold in well-drained blueberries. Fill paper-lined muffin cups 2/3 full and bake 20 to 25 minutes at 375° or until cupcakes test done. Sprinkle with confectioners' sugar. Makes 18 muffins.

* * *

BLUEBERRY CORN MUFFINS

1 (15 oz.) pkg. cornbread mix
1 c. milk
1 egg

1 cup fresh or frozen
  blueberries; thawed,
  rinsed and drained

Make cornbread mix as package label directs, using milk and egg. Gently fold in blueberries. Scoop batter into paper-lined muffin cups and bake about 20 minutes at 425° or until golden brown. Serve hot. Makes 12 muffins.

* * *

BLUEBERRY DESSERT PIZZA

1 pkg. (2 layer size) white
    or yellow cake mix
1 c. quick cooking oats
½ c. butter or margarine,
    softened
¼ c. brown sugar

1 egg
¼ c. coconut
1 tsp. cinnamon
1 (22 oz.) can blueberry
    pie filling
½ c. chopped nuts (optional)

Heat oven to 350°. Grease a 12 or 14-inch pizza pan or a 9x13-inch baking pan. Combine cake mix, oatmeal, and butter or margarine and mix until crumbly. Reserve 1¼ cups and blend 1 egg into remaining crumbs and press into pan. Bake for about 10 minutes. Meanwhile to reserved crumbs add brown sugar, cinnamon, coconut and nuts, if desired. Mix until well blended. Spread pie filling on base and sprinkle with topping. Bake 15 minutes more or until crumbs are light brown. Cool before cutting.

* * *

BLUEBERRY STREUSEL SHORTCAKE

¼ c. plus 3 Tbls. butter
    or margarine
2¼ c. buttermilk biscuit
    mix (divided)
½ c. milk
¼ c. packed brown sugar

3/4 tsp. cinnamon
    (divided)
1 can (22 oz.) blueberry
    pie filling
2 Tbls. lemon juice
    Whipped cream

Cut ¼ cup butter into 2 cups biscuit mix until mixture forms coarse crumbs. Add milk and stir with fork to form soft dough. Spread in greased 8-inch round layer pan. With fork, blend remaining biscuit mix, 3 tablespoons butter, the brown sugar and ¼ teaspoon cinnamon. Sprinkle evenly on dough or spread if too soft to sprinkle. Bake in hot oven (400°) for 20 to 25 minutes. Heat together filling, lemon juice and remaining cinnamon. Cut cake in wedges and serve with hot blueberry sauce and whipped cream. Makes 6 to 8 servings.

* * *

BLUEBERRY-APPLE CRISP

1 pint blueberries, rinsed
   and drained
2 c. tart apples, sliced
   and peeled
1 Tbl. lemon juice
½ c. packed brown sugar
1 c. flour

3/4 c. granulated sugar
1 tsp. baking powder
3/4 tsp. salt
1 egg
1/3 c. butter or margarine,
   melted and cooled
½ tsp. cinnamon

Cream

Butter a 1½-quart baking dish and put in blueberries and apples. Sprinkle with lemon juice and brown sugar. Mix next 4 ingredients, stir in egg and mix until crumbly. Sprinkle over fruit. Top with butter; sprinkle with cinnamon; bake at 350° for 35 to 40 minutes. Serve warm with cream. Makes 6 servings.

* * *

SIMPLE BLUEBERRY ROUNDS

2 c. flour
3 tsp. baking powder
½ tsp. salt
¼ c. sugar
1/3 c. salad oil

½ c. light cream
1 egg
1 c. fresh or frozen
   blueberries, thawed
   and drained

In a medium bowl add flour, baking powder, salt and 2 tablespoons sugar. Add oil and cream all at once. Add egg; stir with a fork until well blended. Gently fold in blueberries and form dough into a ball. Turn dough onto a 12-inch square of waxed paper. Cover with another 12-inch square of waxed paper. Roll out the dough between sheets of waxed paper to form a 10-inch circle. Peel off top sheet and invert on greased cookie sheet. Peel rest of waxed paper off and sprinkle surface evenly with remaining 2 tablespoons sugar. Bake for 20 minutes or until nicely brown at 425°. Serve hot.

* * *

BLUEBERRY LATKES

2 c. sifted flour
3 tsp. baking powder
1 Tbl. sugar
2 Tbls. matzo meal
1½ c. milk

3 eggs, well beaten
4 Tbls. butter or marga-
    rine, melted
2 (10 oz.) pkgs. frozen
    blueberries in syrup

Thaw blueberries. Combine dry ingredients. Combine eggs
and milk; stir into dry ingredients. Stir in melted butter; beat until smooth. Bake latkes like pancakes, using
about 2 tablespoons batter for each, on hot, lightly
greased griddle. To serve, heat fruit gently; spread
latkes with additional butter and put together in stacks
of three with blueberries between and on top. Top with
maple syrup. Makes 6 to 8 servings.

* * *

BLUEBERRY OATMEAL PANCAKES

1 c. pancake mix
1 c. quick cooking oats
2 Tbls. brown sugar
3/4 c. milk

2 eggs
2 Tbls. melted margarine
½ c. fresh blueberries,
    washed and drained

Preheat griddle. Combine all ingredients except blueberries and mix well. Fold in blueberries. Makes 12 to
14 pancakes.

* * *

BLUEBERRY PANCAKE SAUCE

½ c. sugar
1½ tsp. cornstarch
½ c. water
2 tsp. lemon juice

1/8 tsp. nutmeg
Dash of salt
1½ c. blueberries, rinsed
    and drained

Mix all ingredients, except blueberries and lemon juice,
until well blended. Add blueberries and cook over low
heat until sauce is thickened and clear, stirring constantly. Stir in lemon juice. Makes 1½ cups sauce.

* * *

BLUSHING COOKIE TRIANGLES

1 (9 or 11 oz.) pkg. pie
   crust mix
¼ c. sugar
5 to 6 Tbls. cold water

Bama Blueberry Preserves,
   or any other flavor
Bama Preserves
Confectioners' sugar

Preheat oven to 350°. In medium bowl, combine pie crust mix and sugar; mix well. Add water, 1 tablespoon at a time, to form a firm dough. Divide dough in half; shape each into a smooth ball. Roll out on well-floured surface to 1/8-inch thickness. Cut into 2½-inch squares. Place about ½ teaspoon preserves in center of each square. Fold over to make triangles. If desired, seal edges with fork. Bake 15 minutes or until preserves are hot (cookie does not brown). Repeat with remaining dough. Cool. Sprinkle with confectioners' sugar. Makes about 3 dozen.

Reprinted permission of Bama Products.

* * *

BLUEBERRY-FILLED MACAROONS

2½ c. flour
½ tsp. salt
¼ tsp. baking powder
1 c. shortening
½ c. confectioners' sugar
2 tsp. vanilla extract

2 Tbls. milk
2 (8 oz.) cans almond
   paste
2 c. granulated sugar
6 egg whites
1 can (22 oz.) blueberry
   pie filling

In a large bowl mix shortening, confectioners' sugar and vanilla until creamy. Combine flour, salt and baking powder and add to first mixture. Add milk and refrigerate dough until easy to handle.

On lightly floured board, roll dough to 3/8-inch thick and cut into nine 4-inch rounds. Place rounds on cookie sheet 1-inch apart and bake at 350° for 15 minutes. In a medium bowl, stir almond paste with sugar and egg whites until smooth. Spoon into a pastry bag and press mixture into a border around outer edge of each cookie; make another circle inside first one. Fill center of each cookie with about a tablespoon of blueberry pie filling. Bake 20 minutes. Cool and store tightly covered. Makes 9 large cookies. Refrigerate leftover pie filling.

* * *

BLUEBERRY CHEESE CHUBBIES

1 c. all-purpose flour
½ c. butter or margarine
½ of an 8 oz. pkg.
   cream cheese

3/4 c. blueberry pie
   filling
1 egg white, beaten until
   frothy
Granulated sugar

Cut butter and cheese into flour until dough is size of peas. Work dough with hands until it cleans bowl, press firmly into ball. Chill 1 hour. Heat oven to 375°. Roll dough to 1/16-inch thick on floured board. Cut in 5x2½-inch rectangles, spread with 1 teaspoon blueberry pie filling, leaving ½-inch at edges. Roll up carefully, beginning at narrow edge. Seal well by pinching edge. Place pinched edge underneath on ungreased baking sheet, press down slightly. Brush with egg white, sprinkle generously with sugar. Bake about 15 minutes or until slightly brown on top.

* * *

6-LAYER BLUEBERRY SQUARES

1 c. flour
¼ c. confectioners' sugar
¼ c. butter or margarine,
   softened
3 c. fresh blueberries
1 c. sugar
2 Tbls. cornstarch

1½ Tbls. quick tapioca
¼ c. water
1½ c. coconut
1 c. butterscotch chips
½ c. chopped nuts
1 can Eagle Brand Sweetened
   Condensed Milk

Combine flour, confectioners' sugar and butter and pat into a 9x13-inch baking pan. Bake at 350° for 20 minutes. Combine blueberries, sugar, cornstarch, tapioca and water in a large saucepan and simmer until thickened. Set aside to cool. After crust is baked, sprinkle with 3/4 cup coconut; then prepared blueberry mixture as second layer; remaining coconut; butterscotch chips; and chopped nuts. Pour Eagle Brand Sweetened Condensed Milk over top. Bake 30 minutes at 350° and cool completely before cutting.

* * *

BLUEBERRY RIPPLE

1 lg. box vanilla pudding mix $4\frac{1}{2}$ c. fresh blueberries
1 (13 oz.) box vanilla wafers   1 (9 oz.) container frozen
$3\frac{1}{2}$ c. milk   whipped topping, thawed

Cook pudding using $3\frac{1}{2}$ cups milk for a thinner pudding.
While pudding is cooking, arrange $\frac{1}{2}$ the box of vanilla
wafers in a single layer in the bottom of a 9x13-inch
baking pan. Sprinkle about 2 cups blueberries on top
of wafers. Pour about half the pudding over blueberries,
covering all the wafers and blueberries. Repeat the same
for second layer; wafers, blueberries, then pudding.
Refrigerate 2 hours or more. Spread whipped topping over
top before serving and sprinkle with remaining $\frac{1}{2}$ cup
blueberries.

* * *

BLUEBERRY TORTE

$\frac{1}{2}$ c. butter or margarine $1\frac{1}{2}$ c. graham cracker crumbs
1 c. sugar   1 c. all-purpose flour
3 eggs   1 tsp. baking powder
3/4 c. milk   1 tsp. baking soda
1 pint blueberries, washed   2 c. whipping cream
   and drained   Blueberries for garnish

Cream butter or margarine; beat in sugar. Beat in eggs,
one at a time. Stir in milk. Combine 1 pint of blueberries, cracker crumbs, flour, baking powder and baking
soda. Add all at once to first mixture. Mix until well
blended. Pour into greased, floured 8-inch springform
pan. Bake at 375° for 50 to 60 minutes or until cake
tests done. Serve topped with whipped cream sprinkled
with about 3/4 cup blueberries. May be served warm or
cold.

* * *

BLUEBERRY SQUARES

2 c. flour   1 egg
$2\frac{1}{2}$ tsp. baking powder   1 tsp. vanilla extract
$\frac{1}{4}$ tsp. salt $\frac{1}{2}$ c. milk
1/3 c. shortening $1\frac{1}{2}$ c. fresh blueberries,
3/4 c. sugar   washed and drained

Beat shortening with sugar, egg and vanilla until well
blended. Add milk, mixing just until combined. Add flour
along with baking powder and salt; blend 1 minute longer.
Gently fold in blueberries. Turn into greased 9-inch
pan and bake at 375° for 30 minutes or until cake tests
done.

RED, WHITE & BLUEBERRY DELIGHT

1 can Eagle Brand Sweetened
  Condensed Milk
1/3 c. ReaLemon Reconstituted
  Lemon Juice
2 tsp. grated lemon rind
2 c. (16 oz.) plain yogurt
½ c. chopped pecans

2 c. white miniature
  marshmallows
1 pint fresh strawberries,
  sliced and well drained
1 c. fresh or frozen
  blueberries, well
  drained

In large bowl, combine sweetened condensed milk, lemon juice, and rind; mix well. Stir in yogurt, marshmallows and nuts. In 13x9-inch baking pan, spread half of the sweetened condensed milk mixture. Arrange half of the strawberries and blueberries on top, cover with remaining sweetened condensed milk mixture and top with remaining fruit. Cover with foil; freeze until firm. Remove from freezer 10 minutes before cutting.

TIP: Well-drained fruit may be folded into sweetened condensed milk mixture and spread into pan.

Reprinted permission of Borden Eagle Brand Sweetened Condensed Milk and ReaLemon/ReaLime Products.

* * *

BLUEBERRY BUTTERSCOTCH SQUARES

1½ c. all-purpose flour
½ tsp. salt
¼ tsp. baking soda
3/4 c. butter
1 c. granulated sugar

2 eggs
1 to 2 c. blueberries
½ c. butterscotch chips
½ c. chopped pecans
2 Tbls. brown sugar

Mix flour, salt and baking soda. Cream butter until light and fluffy. Gradually beat in sugar. Beat in eggs one at a time. Stir in dry ingredients. Fold in blueberries. Spread mixture into a well-greased 9x13-inch baking pan. Sprinkle with chips, pecans and brown sugar. Bake at 350° for 30 minutes. Top should be lightly browned. Cool in pan.

* * *

FRESH BLUEBERRY TURNOVERS

2 pkgs. pie crust mix
½ c. finely ground pecans
4 tsp. grated lemon rind

3 c. fresh blueberries, rinsed and drained
48 sm. sugar cubes

Additional sugar

Prepare pie crust mix according to package directions, adding pecans and lemon rind; mix before adding water. Knead dough lightly on floured board. Roll out half the dough to an oblong 12x18-inches. Cut dough into 24 3-inch squares. Brush squares lightly with water. Top each square with some blueberries and a sugar cube. Fold over opposite corners and seal. Brush with water and sprinkle with additional sugar. Repeat, using remaining half of the dough. Place turnovers into freezer containers using foil in between layers. Seal and freeze.

When ready to serve, place frozen turnovers on a greased cookie sheet. Bake in a preheated hot oven (400°) for 20 to 25 minutes or until brown. Serve warm or cold. Makes 4 dozen.

NOTE: These turnovers can also be made with blueberry pie filling as long as you omit the sugar cubes.

* * *

BLUEBERRY CRUNCH

1½ c. flour
1 tsp. soda
½ tsp. salt
1 c. quick cooking oats

1 c. packed brown sugar
½ c. butter or margarine, softened
1 (22 oz.) can blueberry pie filling

Combine all ingredients except pie filling, and blend with fingers until fine. Put half the mixture on bottom of a 9x13-inch baking pan. Spread blueberry pie filling over "crust" and add rest of crumbly mixture. Bake at 325° for 50 to 60 minutes.

* * *

BLUEBERRIES FOSTER

2 Tbls. butter or margarine
1 lg. ripe banana, mashed
2 Tbls. sugar
3/4 tsp. cinnamon

3 oz. blackberry or
   raspberry brandy
2 c. fresh blueberries
3 oz. brandy

In chafing dish or skillet, melt butter; add banana.
Mix sugar and cinnamon. Stir mixture into pan. Cook,
stirring frequently until sugar is dissolved. Stir in
blackberry brandy. Add blueberries; cook, stirring lightly
until blueberries are thoroughly coated. Cook over low
heat 5 minutes. Pour brandy slowly into pan so it floats
on top of mixture. Ignite. When flames die down, stir
sauce once and serve immediately over vanilla or blueberry
ripple ice cream. Makes 4 to 6 servings.

* * *

BLUEBERRY CHEESE PARFAITS

1 envelope unflavored gelatine
2 Tbls. ReaLemon Reconstituted
   Lemon Juice
2 Tbls. cold water
1 (16 oz.) container Borden
   Cottage Cheese

$\frac{1}{2}$ c. confectioners' sugar
$\frac{1}{2}$ c. Borden Whipping
   Cream, whipped
1 (22 oz.) can blueberry
   pie filling

In small saucepan, sprinkle gelatine over ReaLemon and
water to soften. Stir over low heat until gelatine dissolves. Cool. In medium bowl, mix cheese and sugar;
stir in gelatine mixture. Fold in whipped cream. Layer
mixture in parfait glasses with blueberry pie filling;
chill. Makes 8 servings.

Reprinted permission of Borden Products and ReaLemon/Rea-
Lime Products.

* * *

BLUEBERRY FLOAT

1 egg
3/4 c. blueberries
2 c. milk

Few drops almond extract
1½ c. whipped cream or whipped topping

Ice cream

Combine egg, blueberries, milk and almond extract in a blender and mix at high speed until smooth. Add whipped cream and gently fold together. Scoop into 6 glasses and top each with ice cream (vanilla or blueberry swirl). Decorate with a few blueberries and enjoy!

* * *

RUMBA COCKTAIL

Combine sliced bananas with mandarin orange segments. Sprinkle with a few blueberries and add light rum to taste.

* * *

BLUEBERRY ICE

1 pint blueberries, washed
½ c. cold water
1 c. granulated sugar

1 c. boiling water
½ c. lemon juice
1 egg white

Place blueberries in container or blender or food processor with cold water and ¼ cup sugar. Blend until mixture is a pureé, and pour into a 1½-quart stainless steel bowl. Combine remaining sugar, boiling water, and lemon juice and stir until sugar is dissolved. Add to blueberry mixture and mix thoroughly.

Beat egg white until stiff, but not dry, and fold into blueberry mixture. Place in coldest part of freezer. When ice begins to form around the edges, stir toward center, checking every half hour and repeating until mixture is slushy. Beat with a rotary egg beater and return to freezer. Repeat at least once more until ice is quite solid. Serve immediately, or pack into quart container; cover and store until needed. Makes 1 quart.

* * *

BLUEBERRY LEMON ICE CREAM

1 c. fresh blueberries
3 egg yolks
1 can sweetened condensed milk

1 Tbl. grated lemon rind
2 c. whipping cream, whipped

Blend blueberries in blender until smooth; set aside. In large bowl, beat egg yolks; stir in sweetened condensed milk and lemon rind. Fold in whipped cream. Add blueberries, gently swirl with knife. Pour into aluminum foil-lined 9x5-inch loaf pan or other 2-quart container; cover. Freeze 6 hours or until firm. Scoop ice cream from pan or remove from pan, peel off foil and slice.

* * *

BLUEBERRY 'N' SPICE SAUCE

$\frac{1}{2}$ c. sugar
1 Tbl. cornstarch
$\frac{1}{2}$ tsp. cinnamon

$\frac{1}{4}$ tsp. nutmeg
$\frac{1}{2}$ c. hot water
2 c. fresh blueberries

Wash and drain blueberries. In small saucepan, combine sugar, cornstarch, cinnamon and nutmeg. Gradually stir in water. Cook, stirring constantly, over low heat until mixture thickens and comes to a boil. Stir in blueberries; cook, stirring constantly until mixture comes again to a boil. Simmer 5 minutes. Serve warm over ice cream or cake. Refrigerate leftovers.

* * *

BLUEBERRY ICE CREAM MUFFINS

$1\frac{1}{2}$ c. flour
1 Tbl. baking powder
1 tsp. salt
2 Tbls. sugar

1 egg
2 Tbls. cooking oil
2 c. vanilla ice cream, softened

1 cup blueberries

Combine dry ingredients; add remaining ingredients, except blueberries. Beat until smooth. Fold in washed and well-drained blueberries. Fill well-greased muffin tins 3/4 full. Bake at 425° for 20 to 25 minutes, or until golden brown. Makes 12 muffins.

* * *

BLUEBERRY SURPRISE CANDIES

72 firm blueberries
3/4 c. mashed potatoes
1 pound flaked coconut
  (about 4 cups)

1 lb. confectioners'
  sugar (about 3 3/4 cups)
1 tsp. almond extract
  Chocolate coating*

Combine potatoes, coconut, sugar, and extract in large mixing bowl. Pick up heaping teaspoonful, and mold around each blueberry. Roll into balls, refrigerate ½ to 1 hour. If mixture is too soft to form balls, refrigerate first, then shape. Dip balls in coating. Place on waxed paper and refrigerate to harden.

*CHOCOLATE COATING: Mix 2 tablespoons soft butter, 2 tablespoons corn syrup, and 3 tablespoons water in top of double boiler. Stir in 1 package fudge flavor frosting mix until smooth. Heat over rapidly boiling water 5 minutes, stirring occasionally.

* * *

BLUEBERRY-CHEESE DESSERT

2½ c. graham cracker crumbs
½ c. sugar
½ c. margarine
2 eggs

1½ c. sugar
1 (8 oz.) pkg. cream cheese
1 can (22 oz.) blueberry
  pie filling

Melt margarine in a 9x13-inch baking pan, add ½ cup sugar and graham cracker crumbs; mix with a fork and press down to make the crust. Soften cream cheese, add eggs and remaining sugar, beating until creamy. Pour onto crust. Bake 35 minutes at 325°; cool. Spread blueberry pie filling over cheese mixture and top with whipped cream, if desired, when ready to serve.

* * *

RED, WHITE, AND BLUEBERRY TARTS

Baked 3-inch tart shells
1 (3¼ oz.) pkg. vanilla
    pudding mix
1 3/4 c. milk
2 c. fresh blueberries,
    rinsed and drained

½ of a can (22 oz.) blue-
    berry pie filling
1 tsp. pumpkin pie spice
Juice of 1 lemon
Whipped topping or cream
Maraschino cherries

Prepare vanilla pudding mix according to package directions using only 1 3/4 cup milk. Cover and cool. Divide
mixture among tarts. Top with fresh blueberries. Combine
blueberry pie filling, pumpkin pie spice and lemon juice.
Spoon mixture over fresh blueberries in tarts. Decorate
with whipped topping and cherries. Makes 6 tarts.

* * *

BLUEBERRY CREAM PUFFS

1 c. water
½ c. butter or margarine
1 c. flour
4 eggs

1 can (22 oz.) blueberry
    pie filling
2 c. whipped topping
½ c. coconut

Heat water and butter to full boil and stir flour in all
at once. Beat hard over low heat about 1 minute or until
mixture forms a ball. Remove from heat; beat in eggs
one at a time, beating until smooth. Drop dough by scant
1/3 cupfuls onto ungreased baking sheet. Bake in hot
oven (400°) for 35 to 40 minutes or until puffed, dry
and nicely brown. Remove from baking sheet and cool.
Cut off tops and remove excess webbing.

Set aside ½ cup blueberry pie filling and fold whipped
topping and coconut into remaining pie filling; fill cream
puffs, using about ½ cup filling mixture for each. Cover
with tops and spoon reserved ½ cup pie filling over tops.
Makes 8 cream puffs.

* * *

When you spread a bit of blueberry jam on breakfast toast, you are treating yourself like Scottish royalty.

Blueberry jam, the story goes, was invented in the court of James V. His French wife, Madeleine, brought her own cooks when she arrived at the castle in Scotland. The cooks harvested the local wild berries for a jam to wake up the court's tired palates.

* * *

ROYAL BLUEBERRY JAM

1½ quarts blueberries   7 c. sugar
1 lemon   1 (6 oz.) bottle pectin

Crush berries.* Grate rind of lemon; juice the lemon. Add rind and juice to berries. Add sugar and mix well. Place over high heat and bring to a full rolling boil. Boil hard for 1 minute, stirring constantly. Remove from heat and add liquid pectin. Stir and skim off foam for 5 minutes. Ladle immediately into hot, sterilized jars and seal at once with paraffin. Makes 12 (8 oz.) jars.

*NOTE: If you have a food grinder, use that to crush the blueberries. I have an Oster Kitchen Center and used the grinder part to help me with my blueberry jam last August. It worked beautifully!

* * *

BLUEBERRY JAM

1½ quarts blueberries   4 c. sugar
1 lemon   1 box powder fruit jel

Wash and drain blueberries. Crush berries, one layer at a time, and add juice of 1 lemon and powdered fruit jel. Place over high heat and stir until mixture comes to a boil. Add sugar and bring to a rolling boil; boil hard for 1 minute, stirring constantly. Remove from heat; skim off foam and ladle into hot, sterilized jars and seal at once with paraffin.

* * *

CRANBERRIES

CRANBERRY-SAUCED HAM ROLLS

½ c. chopped onions
½ c. sliced celery
½ c. butter or margarine
    Cranberry Sauce Topping*

4 c. cooked rice
Salt and pepper
16 ham slices

Melt butter or margarine in a medium saucepan and sauté onions and celery until tender. Stir in rice and season to taste with salt and pepper. Place ¼ cup of rice mixture on a thin slice of cooked ham. Roll up and place, seam side down, in a buttered roasting pan. Repeat with 15 more ham slices. Spoon 1 tablespoon cranberry sauce over each ham roll and bake at 350° until thoroughly heated, about 20 minutes. When serving, pour a little more warm sauce over each ham roll.

*CRANBERRY SAUCE TOPPING: Melt 2 cans whole cranberry sauce. Add ½ cup firmly packed brown sugar and ¼ cup lemon juice.

* * *

BAKED HAM SLICES WITH CRANBERRY GLAZE

4 pound Swift Premium Hostess
  Ham in round can
½ c. sugar
½ tsp. nutmeg

1 Tbl. cornstarch
1 c. cranberry juice
  cocktail
½ c. whole cranberries

Open both ends of round can and remove ham. Cut into slices ¼ to ½ inch thick. Arrange ham slices in baking dish. Ladle glaze over slices and bake in a moderate oven (350°F.), 15 minutes. Serve hot.

TO MAKE GLAZE: In a saucepan combine sugar, nutmeg and cornstarch. Add cranberry juice and bring to a boil, stirring constantly. Add whole cranberries and bring to a boil once more. Yield: 1½ cups glaze.

Reprinted permission of Swift & Company.

* * *

CRANBERRY-ORANGE WALNUT STUFFING

¼ c. finely chopped onion
¼ c. finely chopped celery
½ stick (¼ c.) butter or
   margarine
½ c. cut-up orange sections
½ c. chopped raw cranberries
2 Tbls. water

½ c. chopped walnuts
2 Tbls. sugar
½ tsp. poultry seasoning
¼ tsp. salt
4 c. dry bread cubes
1 egg, beaten

Sauté onion and celery in butter until tender. Add orange, cranberries, and walnuts. Combine sugar and seasonings and sprinkle over bread cubes. Add cranberry mixture, egg and water. Toss mixture lightly with forks until bread cubes are well moistened. Stuff thawed, rinsed turkey and roast immediately. Makes 4½ cups (enough for a 6 to 7 pound Li'L Butterball Turkey).

Reprinted permission of Swift & Company.

* * *

CRANBERRY-BARBECUE SAUCE

8 oz. can cranberry sauce
1/3 c. catsup
2 Tbls. brown sugar

2 Tbls. butter or
   margarine
1/8 tsp. garlic powder

Combine ingredients in a small saucepan. Heat and stir until cranberry sauce is dissolved. Brush over turkey several times during last half hour of cooking. Serve remaining sauce with turkey.

Reprinted permission of Swift & Company.

* * *

CRANBERRY HONEY GLAZE

16 oz. can whole cranberry
   sauce

½ c. honey
1 Tbl. lemon juice

Combine cranberry sauce, honey and lemon juice in small saucepan. Cook over low heat stirring constantly until cranberry sauce is melted. Spoon glaze over turkey during last half hour of cooking time. Serve any remaining sauce with sliced turkey.

Reprinted permission of Swift & Company.

* * *

CRANBERRY SALAD CROWN

2 envelopes unflavored gelatin
$2\frac{1}{2}$ c. cocktail vegetable juice
1 (8 oz.) can jellied
   sauce
$\frac{1}{2}$ c. raisins
$\frac{1}{2}$ c. orange juice

$\frac{1}{2}$ c. sliced celery
$\frac{1}{2}$ c. orange sections, diced
$\frac{1}{2}$ c. chopped walnuts
$\frac{1}{2}$ c. crushed pineapple,*
   well drained
Sour cream

In saucepan, sprinkle gelatin over vegetable juice to soften; add cranberry sauce and raisins. Place over low heat, stirring until gelatin dissolves; add orange juice. Chill until slightly thickened. Fold in remaining ingredients, except sour cream. Pour into 5 cup mold; chill until firm. Unmold on salad greens. Serve with sour cream.

      *Do not use fresh or frozen pineapple

* * *

FROZEN CRANBERRY SALAD

$1\frac{1}{2}$ c. canned crushed pineapple, well drained
1 can whole cranberry sauce

1 c. sour cream
$\frac{1}{4}$ c. nuts, coarsely chopped
Sour cream

Combine all ingredients except sour cream and pour into an 8-inch square pan. Freeze overnight. Serve on lettuce leaves with a dollop of sour cream, if desired.

* * *

MOLDED CRANBERRY SAUCE

2 c. sugar
2 c. water

4 c. fresh
   cranberries

Combine sugar and water in large saucepan and heat to boiling; boil 5 minutes. Add cranberries and continue cooking another 15 minutes or until a drop of sauce jells on a cold plate. Pour into a 4-cup mold and chill until firm.

* * *

CRANBERRIES 'N' SOUR CREAM

For a quick delicious dessert, serve chilled, sweetened, stewed cranberries with sour cream and a sprinkling of grated fresh ginger!

* * *

CRANBERRY-BAKED APPLES

6 lg. baking apples
3/4 c. chopped raw
   cranberries

3 Tbls. chopped nuts
$\frac{1}{2}$ c. sugar
$\frac{1}{2}$ c. water

Wash and core apples. Pare apples one-third of the way down or slit the skin around the apple about half-way down. Place apples in a baking dish. Combine cranberries, sugar and chopped nuts. Stuff apples with this mixture. Pour the water around apples to prevent sticking. Bake, uncovered, at 400° until tender, about 45 to 60 minutes.

* * *

CRANBERRY-APPLE RINGS

6 apples, cored and sliced
2 c. cranberries
1 c. maple-flavored syrup

$\frac{1}{2}$ tsp. cinnamon
2 Tbls. butter or margarine
Cream

Arrange apple rings (peeled, if desired) in shallow 2-quart baking dish, overlapping slices to fit. Top with cranberries. Sprinkle with cinnamon, add syrup and dot with butter. Cover and bake for $1\frac{1}{2}$ hours at 350° or until fruit is tender. Baste several times while baking. Serve warm with cream.

* * *

MOLDED CRAN-APPLE SALAD

1 lg. pkg. strawberry gelatin
1 can (1 lb.) whole cran-
   berry sauce
2 c. boiling water

1 can (1 lb.) pears, drained
1 c. sliced celery
1 lg. red apple, cored
   and chopped

Place gelatin in large bowl, add boiling water and stir until dissolved. Stir in cranberry sauce and chill until slightly thickened. Cut pears in large chunks and fold into gelatin mixture along with celery and apple. Pour into a 6-cup mold and chill until firm (3 to 4 hours).

* * *

ZIPPY CRANBERRY SAUCE

1 can (1 lb.) whole cran-
   berry sauce

1 tsp. worcestershire
1 tsp. orange peel

Combine ingredients in bowl, blend well. Chill before serving. Makes 2 cups. Serve with pork or chicken.

* * *

SNOWY COCONUT COTTAGE RING

1½ envelopes unflavored gelatine
1½ c. cold water
2 (16 oz.) containers Borden
  Cottage Cheese
1 (14 oz.) can Eagle Brand
  Sweetened Condensed Milk
1 (3½ oz.) can flaked
  coconut
Lettuce leaves
Whole Cranberry Sauce OR
2 to 3 c. mixed fresh
  fruits

In small saucepan, sprinkle gelatine over water to soften; stir over low heat until gelatine dissolves; cool. In large bowl, combine cheese, sweetened condensed milk and coconut; mix well. Stir in gelatine. Turn into lightly oiled 1½-quart ring mold. Chill 4 hours or until firm. Unmold onto lettuce; fill center with whole berry cranberry sauce or fresh fruit. Refrigerate. Makes 12 servings.

Reprinted permission of Borden Products.

* * *

CRANBERRY ORANGE SALAD

1 (3 oz.) pkg. strawberry
  gelatin
1 c. boiling water
3/4 c. cold water
½ orange, unpeeled
2 c. raw cranberries
1 apple, diced
3 Tbls. sugar

Dissolve gelatin in boiling water; add cold water. Chill until thickened. Cut up orange wedges and remove seeds. Put orange and cranberries through grinder; mix in apple and sugar. Fold in thickened gelatin. Pour into 3-cup ring mold or individual molds. Chill until firm.

* * *

CRANBERRY GELATIN RING

2 apples, peeled and cored
1 seedless orange, unpeeled
1½ c. raw
  cranberries
½ c. sugar
1 pkg. (3 oz.) raspberry
  gelatin
1 c. boiling water

Cut apples and oranges in chunks or put through coarse blade of grinder with cranberries. Dissolve gelatin and sugar in boiling water. Chill slightly. Stir in fruit. Pour into mold and chill until set.

* * *

CRANBERRY ROUND MOLD

1 quart cranberries
2 apples, chopped
2 c. sugar
1 envelope unflavored
    gelatin
¼ c. cold water

1 (3 oz.) pkg. lemon
    gelatin
½ c. boiling water
Grated rind of 1 orange
1 c. orange juice
Mayonnaise

Grind cranberries, add chopped apples and sugar. Soften unflavored gelatin in cold water; heat until gelatin dissolves and add to cranberry-apple mixture. Dissolve lemon gelatin in boiling water, add rind and juice. Mix everything together and pour into 8-cup greased ring mold. Let stand overnight; turn out onto bed of lettuce and fill center with mayonnaise.

* * *

CRANBERRY HEAVENLY HASH

1½ c. cranberries, finely
    chopped
½ c. sugar
1 c. miniature marshmallows
1 c. chopped nuts

4 bananas, sliced
2 cans pineapple tidbits,
    drained
2 c. whipping cream, whipped
1 tsp. rum extract

Combine cranberries and sugar and mix well. Stir in next 4 ingredients; then fold in whipped cream and rum extract. Chill several hours. Keeps well several days.

* * *

CRANBERRY RELISH

4 c. fresh cranberries,
    ground
2 tart cooking apples,
    peeled, cored and ground

1 3/4 c. sugar
½ c. chopped walnuts
2 drops red
    food coloring

Combine first 3 ingredients, mixing well. Add remaining ingredients stirring until blended. Chill. Store in air tight container in refrigerator. Makes 1 quart.

* * *

CRANBERRY BUTTER

4 c. fresh cranberries,
  washed
2/3 c. water
½ c. Heinz Apple Cider OR
  Apple Cider Flavored
  Distilled Vinegar
2 c. firmly packed light
  brown sugar

½ tsp. ground cinnamon
½ tsp. salt
¼ tsp. pepper
¼ tsp. allspice
¼ tsp. nutmeg
2 Tbls. butter or
  margarine

Combine first 3 ingredients in saucepan; boil 5 minutes; cool. Pureé mixture in food processor, blender or food mill; return to saucepan. Stir in brown sugar and next 5 ingredients. Simmer 3 minutes, stirring occasionally. Stir in butter. Pour mixture into bowl; cover and chill. Serve as a meat accompaniment. Makes about 3½ cups.

Reprinted with permission of H. J. Heinz Co..

* * *

SPICED CRANBERRIES

1 1/3 c. Heinz Distilled White
  Vinegar
2/3 c. water
4 c. granulated sugar

4 tsp. ground ginger
1 tsp. ground cloves
2 quarts (2 lb.) fresh
  cranberries, washed

Combine first 5 ingredients in saucepot; heat to boiling. Add cranberries; simmer 25 minutes, stirring occasionally. Continue simmering while quickly packing one clean, hot jar at a time. Fill to within ½ inch of top making sure vinegar solution covers cranberries. Cap each jar at once. Process 5 minutes in boiling water bath. Makes 3 to 4 pints.

Reprinted permission of H. J. Heinz Co..

* * *

CRANBERRY PICKLE SAUCE

4 c. fresh cranberries
1½ c. sugar
½ c. vinegar

½ tsp. cinnamon
½ tsp. nutmeg
½ tsp. cloves

Combine cranberries, sugar and vinegar; allow to come slowly to a boil. Cook until all cranberries burst. Add spices. Cook over low heat for 15 minutes. Reduce heat to simmer the last 5 minutes of cooking. Pour into hot pint jars. Adjust lids at once. Process in boiling water bath for 5 minutes. Remove from canner and complete seal.

BAKED CRANBERRY PUDDING I

2 c. fresh cranberries, cut $1\frac{1}{4}$ c. flour
$\frac{1}{2}$ c. hot water $\frac{1}{2}$ tsp. salt
1/3 c. molasses   2 tsp. soda
$\frac{1}{4}$ c. dark corn syrup   Sauce*

To the cranberries, add hot water, molasses and dark corn syrup. Combine dry ingredients and add to cranberry mixture. Blend well. Bake at 375° for 25 minutes in a 9-inch square pan. Serve warm with the following sauce.

*SAUCE: Combine 1 cup light cream, 1 cup sugar and $\frac{1}{2}$ cup margarine in a small saucepan and bring to a boil, cooking for 3 minutes. Add 1 teaspoon vanilla or rum extract.

* * *

BAKED CRANBERRY PUDDING II

2 c. cranberries, cut $\frac{1}{2}$ c. raisins
$\frac{1}{4}$ c. sugar   1 1/3 c. flour
$\frac{1}{2}$ c. molasses   1 tsp. soda
$\frac{1}{2}$ c. hot water   Dash of salt

Grease and flour 11x7-inch baking pan. Combine all ingredients in order given and pour into pan. Bake for 45 minutes at 350°. Serve with the following sauce...

SAUCE: Cook in double boiler scant $\frac{1}{2}$ cup margarine, $\frac{1}{2}$ cup sugar and $\frac{1}{2}$ cup light cream. Serve over warm cranberry pudding. Pudding may be made ahead of time and reheated in oven.

* * *

QUICK CRANBERRY BANANA DESSERT

Top sliced bananas with cubes of jellied cranberry sauce. Top with whipped cream and chopped nuts.

* * *

CRANBERRY DESSERT

1 lb. cranberries, ground   1 c. small marshmallows
1 can crushed pineapple,   1 c. whipping cream,
   drained   whipped
1 c. sugar $\frac{1}{2}$ c. chopped nuts

Mix first three ingredients and let stand overnight. Combine remaining ingredients, mix well and chill.

Dorothy Srock

* * *

CRANBERRY REFRIGERATOR DESSERT

2 c. cranberries
1 lg. banana, diced
½ c. sugar
1 c. whipping cream,
    whipped

2 c. vanilla wafer crumbs
6 Tbls. melted butter
½ c. margarine
1 c. sugar
2 eggs

Grind cranberries and combine with banana and ½ cup sugar.
Set aside. Combine wafer crumbs and melted butter. Press
half the crumb mixture in a 9-inch square pan. Cream
½ cup margarine and remaining 1 cup sugar until light.
Add eggs and beat until fluffy. Spread on crumbs. Top
with cranberry mixture; then with whipped cream; sprinkle
with remaining crumbs. Chill 6 hours.

Dorothy Srock

* * *

CRANBERRY SHERBET I

1 (16 oz.) can jellied
    cranberry sauce
2¼ c. water

1 (6 oz.) can frozen
    lemonade concentrate,
    thawed

With egg beater, beat all ingredients until well blended.
Pour into 8-inch square pan and freeze until mushy. Beat
again until smooth and freeze until firm.

* * *

CRANBERRY SHERBET II

1 envelope unflavored
    gelatin
1 can whole cranberry sauce
½ c. water

1 c. orange juice
2 Tbls. sugar
½ tsp. grated orange
    peel

In a small saucepan, sprinkle gelatin over water and cook,
stirring constantly until dissolved. Cool slightly.
In blender, whirl dissolved gelatin, cranberry sauce,
orange juice and sugar until smooth (only a few seconds).
Pour into a 9x13-inch pan and freeze until slushy in center. Pour into chilled bowl and beat at high speed until
mixture becomes a lighter color and texture. Stir in
orange peel. Freeze until firm.

* * *

CRANBERRY CUPCAKES

1/3 c. butter	1 tsp. baking powder
2/3 c. sugar	½ tsp. baking soda
2 eggs	¼ tsp. salt
½ c. cooked cranberries	1½ c. flour
1 Tbl. grated orange rind	Pecans

Cream butter and sugar; add eggs and beat well. Add cranberries and orange rind, stir. Slowly add flour, baking powder, soda and salt, stirring constantly. Beat until smooth and creamy. Heat oven to 400°. Fill paper-lined muffin cups 2/3 full and bake 20 to 25 minutes or until golden brown. Frost with Cranberry Frosting*.

*CRANBERRY FROSTING

1 c. confectioners' sugar	1 Tbl. soft butter
1 Tbl. grated orange rind	1 Tbl. cranberry juice

Combine above ingredients and beat until smooth. After frosting cupcakes, decorate each with a pecan half.

* * *

CRANBERRY-ORANGE NUT BREAD

1 c. fresh cranberries, thick sliced	3/4 c. orange juice
2 c. all-purpose flour	1 Tbl. orange peel
1 c. sugar	4 Tbls. soft shortening
1 tsp. salt	1 egg, slightly beaten
1½ tsp. baking powder	1 c. whole pecans or walnuts
½ tsp. baking soda	

Preheat oven to 350°. Assemble Salad Maker. Slice cranberries as indicated above. Assemble Mixer. In large mixer bowl, combine dry ingredients. Add juice, peel, shortening and egg. Mix at #3 until well blended. Stir in nuts and cranberries. Pour into a greased 9x5x3-inch pan. Bake 55 to 60 minutes. Cool slightly before removing from pan. Finish cooling on wire rack. Yield: 1 loaf.

Recipe Courtesy Oster.

CRANBERRY SWIRL COFFEE CAKE

½ c. margarine
1 c. sugar
2 eggs
1 tsp. baking powder
1 tsp. baking soda
2 c. flour

½ tsp. salt
1 c. sour cream
1 tsp. almond flavoring
1 (7 oz.) can whole
   cranberry sauce
½ c. crushed nuts

Cream margarine and sugar at medium speed on electric mixer. Sift dry ingredients and add alternately with sour cream, beginning and ending with dry ingredients. Add flavoring. Put layer of batter in bottom of greased 8-inch tube pan. Swirl ½ of cranberry sauce over batter. Add remaining batter and swirl remaining cranberry sauce over top. Sprinkle with crushed nuts. Bake at 350° for 55 minutes. Remove from pan when slightly cool (approximately 5 minutes) and add topping.

TOPPING: Combine ½ teaspoon almond flavoring, 3/4 cup confectioners' sugar and 1 tablespoon warm water. Spread on top of cake and allow some to run over sides.

* * *

CRANBERRY CRISP COFFEE CAKE

1½ c. KELLOGG'S Sugar Frosted
   Flakes of Corn cereal,
   crushed to 3/4 cup
1 Tbl. margarine or butter,
   melted
1½ c. all-purpose flour
2 tsp. baking powder

½ tsp. salt
¼ c. butter or margarine,
   softened
3/4 c. sugar
1 egg
½ c. milk
1 c. whole cranberry sauce

Mix crushed cereal with melted margarine. Set aside. Stir together flour, baking powder, and salt. Set aside. Beat the ¼ cup margarine, the sugar and egg until well blended. Add milk alternately with flour mixture, mixing well until smooth. Spread batter in greased 9-inch round cake pan. Top evenly with cranberry sauce. Sprinkle with cereal mixture. Bake at 350° for about 50 minutes. Serve warm or cooled. Makes 8 servings.

Reprinted permission of KELLOGG'S Products.

* * *

CRANBERRY APPLE PIE

Pastry for 2 crust 9-in. pie
$2\frac{1}{2}$ c. cranberries, chopped
$1\frac{1}{2}$ c. apples, chopped
$1\frac{1}{2}$ c. sugar
3 Tbls. quick tapioca
3 Tbls. water

Combine all ingredients and let stand while rolling pastry. Fill pie shell and cover with lattice strips. Flute edge. Bake at 425° for 30 to 40 minutes.

* * *

CAPE COD CRANBERRY PIE

1 lb. (4 c.) fresh cranberries
$2\frac{1}{2}$ c. sugar
1/3 c. quick-cooking tapioca
1 tsp. ground cinnamon
$\frac{1}{2}$ tsp. salt
1/8 tsp. ground cloves
$\frac{1}{2}$ c. orange juice
1 c. orange sections, diced
$\frac{1}{2}$ tsp. vanilla extract
1 pkg. (10 or 11 oz.) pie crust mix
1 Tbl. butter or margarine

In a medium saucepan, combine cranberries with sugar, tapioca, cinnamon, salt and cloves. Stir in orange juice. Cover and cook over medium heat until skins pop, about 6 to 8 minutes. Remove from heat; cool slightly. Stir in orange sections and vanilla extract.

Prepare pastry according to package directions. Roll half of the pastry 1/8-inch thick. Use to line a 9-inch pie plate. Turn cranberry mixture into pie shell. Dot with butter. Roll remaining pastry to same thickness. Cut into $\frac{1}{2}$-inch strips; arrange over pie in lattice fashion. Trim and flute edges. Bake in a preheated hot oven (450°) for 10 minutes. Reduce heat to moderate (350°) and bake 20 to 25 minutes longer or until crust is nicely brown.

* * *

CRANBERRY CHEESE CRUNCH PIE

1 (8 oz.) pkg. cream cheese, softened
1 (16 oz.) can whole cran-berry sauce
Unbaked 9-inch pie shell
Brown sugar
3 Tbls. cornstarch
Dash of salt
1/3 c. flour
$\frac{1}{4}$ c. butter or margarine

Blend cream cheese with $\frac{1}{2}$ c. cranberry sauce and spread in pie shell. Mix $\frac{1}{2}$ c. packed brown sugar, cornstarch and salt. Mix with remaining cranberry sauce and pour into shell. Mix flour, 3 tablespoons brown sugar and butter to a crumbly consistency. Sprinkle on pie and bake in preheated 375° oven for about 40 minutes; cool, then refrigerate.

46

FRESH CRANBERRY CHEESE PIE

CRUMB CRUST: Finely crush or put through food chopper (fine blade) 30 lemon wafer cookies (1½ cups crumbs). Blend with ¼ cup melted butter or margarine. Press into bottom and sides of 8-inch pie plate. Chill.

FILLING:

2 (3 oz.) pkgs. cream cheese, softened
1½ tsp. unflavored gelatine
2 Tbls. cold water
1 egg yolk
½ c. sweetened condensed milk (NOT evaporated)

¼ tsp. salt
1 tsp. grated orange rind
½ tsp. Durkee Vanilla
1 egg white
1 c. Durkee Shredded Coconut

Soften gelatine in cold water, then dissolve over hot water. Beat cream cheese until fluffy. Add egg yolk, condensed milk, salt, orange rind and vanilla. Beat well. Stir in dissolved gelatine. Beat egg white until stiff but not dry. Gently fold into cheese mixture. Pour into crumb crust. Chill until firm.

TOPPING: Soften 1½ teaspoons unflavored gelatine in 2 tablespoons cold water; dissolve over hot water. Stir into 1½ cups Cranberry-Orange Relish. Spread on top of cheese mixture. Garnish with coconut.

CRANBERRY-ORANGE RELISH: Put 4 cups (1 lb.) fresh cranberries and 2 oranges (quartered and seeds removed) through food chopper (coarse blade). Stir in 2 cups sugar and chill. Use 1½ cups relish for pie. Save remaining 2½ cups to serve with chicken, turkey or pork.

Reprinted permission of Durkee Famous Foods.

* * *

MOCK CHERRY PIE
(Cranberries)

Pastry for 1 double crust 9-inch pie
1½ c. cranberries (washed and cut in half)
1 c. sugar

1 tsp. vanilla
1 Tbl. flour dissolved in ½ c. water
1 egg, well beaten

Combine all ingredients and mix together well. Bake at 450° for 10 minutes, then lower oven temperature to 350° for about 30 to 40 minutes longer.

* * *

CRANBERRY WINE

8 quarts (12 ½ lbs.)   4 pkgs. dry yeast
   cranberries   2 pieces toast
4 gallons water   15 lbs. sugar
          10 gallon crock

Combine cranberries and water and bring to a boil; boil until cranberries pop; about 5 minutes. Add sugar and pour into a 10-gallon crock. Let cool. Mash cranberries with hands. Put 4 packages yeast on toast and float in crock. After 15 days, remove taost, strain and put in jugs for 10 days, capped loosely.

* * *

CRANBERRY COOLER

3/4 c. cranberry juice   1 tsp. lemon juice
3 oz. gin   1½ c. crushed ice

Assemble Blender. Put all ingredients into blender container. Cover and process at FRAPPE (LIQUEFY) until of sherbet consistency. Mound into glasses and serve with straws. Yield: 4 (3 oz.) drinks.

Recipe Courtesy Oster.

* * *

CRANBERRY COLADA

3 oz. CocoRibe Liqueur   Orange wedge
     3 oz. Cranberry juice cocktail

Pour CocoRibe and cranberry juice over ice in a tall glass and shake. Squeeze orange wedge into glass. Stir.

Recipe courtesy CocoRibe Company.

* * *

*Going back to nature? Try Pear Cranberry Leather.
It is a popular "natural" chewy candy-like fruit snack!*

PEAR CRANBERRY LEATHER

2 lbs. fresh pears   ¼ c. honey
    1 pkg. (12 oz.) fresh cranberries

Cook cranberries in saucepan with small amount of water just until skins pop. Remove from heat and drain well. Cook pears in saucepan with water until tender. Drain. Assemble Pureer. Pureé pears and cranberries into large bowl. Mix well with honey. Pour mixture onto 2 plastic wrap lined 15½x10½x1-inch jelly roll pans. Spread evenly. Bake at 250° until no longer wet to touch, about 4 hours. Remove plastic wrap and cut each sheet into 4 strips. Roll lengthwise and wrap in plastic wrap. Store in refrigerator. Yield: 8 strips.

NOTE: Fruit leathers also may be dried in a dehydrator, following manufacturer's directions.

Recipe Courtesy Oster.

* * *

Candied Cranberries is a sugary-tart candy that was a favorite of all kids when commercial candies weren't available.

CANDIED CRANBERRIES

2 c. fresh cranberries   ½ c. confectioners'
2 egg whites   sugar

Freeze cranberries, uncovered for about 15 minutes. Beat the egg whites lightly, and pour into a shallow bowl. Put the sugar on a plate. Dip the "frost-bitten" cranberries, one by one, in the egg whites, and then roll gently in the confectioners' sugar, until well coated. Put the berries on a foil-covered cookie sheet. Preheat oven to 200° and dry the berries slowly in the oven, leaving the door open, for about 1½ hours, until the egg and sugar form a firm coating. Cool. Serve as candy or use to decorate desserts.

* * *

CRANBERRY UPSIDE-DOWN CAKE

2 c. fresh cranberries
½ c. sugar
½ c. chopped pecans
1 c. sugar

2 eggs
3/4 c. shortening
1 c. flour
Whipping cream, whipped

Wash and drain cranberries; combine with ½ cup sugar and pecans. Spread evenly in greased 10-inch pie plate. Cream eggs, 1 cup sugar and shortening together; stir in flour. Pour over cranberry mixture and bake in pre-heated oven (325°) for 30 to 35 minutes. Serve topped with whipped cream.

* * *

CRANBERRY-ORANGE RELISH

4 c. fresh cranberries
2 c. sugar
½ c. water

1 tsp. grated orange peel
½ c. orange juice
½ c. slivered almonds

Combine all ingredients, except almonds, in a medium sauce-pan and cook, uncovered, for 10 minutes or until cranberry skins pop, stirring occasionally. Remove from heat, stir in almonds and cool. Store in refrigerator.

* * *

CRANBERRY JELLY

3½ c. cranberry juice
   cocktail

4 c. sugar
¼ c. lemon juice

1 pkg. (2½ oz.) powdered fruit pectin

In large saucepan, combine cranberry juice and pectin. Stir over high heat until cranberry mixture comes to a full rolling boil. Stir in sugar all at once. Bring to a full boil again and boil hard for 2 minutes, stirring constantly. Remove from heat, stir in lemon juice and skim foam. Pour into hot scalded jars. Makes 6 (8 oz.) jars of jelly.

* * *

RASPBERRIES

RASPBERRY MALLOWSICLES

2/3 c. evaporated milk   1 Tbl. lemon juice
4½ oz. marshmallow creme   1½ c. fresh raspberries

Freeze all but 3 tablespoons of evaporated milk in refrigerator tray until ice crystals form around edges. Beat
together marshmallow creme, reserved 3 tablespoons of
milk and lemon juice until smooth. Transfer partially
frozen milk to a chilled mixing bowl. Beat until stiff
peaks form. Fold in marshmallow creme mixture and raspberries. Spoon about 1/3 cup mixture into each of 12
3 oz. waxed paper drinking cups. Place in freezer. When
mixture is partially frozen, insert wooden sticks. Freeze
until firm. To serve, peel off paper wrapping. Makes
12 mallowsicles.

* * *

RASPBERRY/BANANA CREAMSICLES

3 c. buttermilk   ¼ c. sugar
2 c. fresh raspberries   1 ripe banana

Blend all ingredients together in blender. Pour into
popsicle molds and freeze until solid. Makes approximately 12 'sicles.

* * *

BRANDIED RASPBERRY BOMBE

¼ c. brandy   1 qt. chocolate ice cream
1 pt. raspberries, washed   Chocolate chips
   and drained   1 c. whipping cream
1 qt. vanilla ice cream   3 drops red food coloring

Pour brandy over raspberries and let stand several hours.
Soften vanilla ice cream; mold to form shell about 3/4
inch thick in a 1½ quart bowl. Freeze firm. Soften chocolate ice cream. Gently fold in raspberries and brandy.
Spoon into vanilla shell. Cover; freeze firm. Unmold.
Whip cream; tint with red food coloring. Decorate bombe
with whipped cream and chocolate chips. Serve immediately.

* * *

BERRY-CHEESE SALAD

1 (8 oz.) carton cream-
    style cottage cheese
1 sm. can pineapple tid-
    bits, drained

½ c. fresh raspberries
½ c. fresh strawberries,
    halved
Lettuce leaves

Combine cottage cheese and pineapple. Arrange washed lettuce leaves on individual serving dishes and mount each with about ½ cup cottage cheese mixture. Top with raspberries and strawberries. Makes 4 servings.

* * *

RASPBERRY CREAM MOLD

1 lg. pkg. raspberry
    gelatin
2 c. boiling water
¼ c. lemon juice
½ c. mayonnaise or
    salad dressing

3 (10 oz.) pkgs. frozen
    raspberries, thawed
1 sm. carton frozen
    whipped topping
1 c. miniature
    marshmallows

Dissolve gelatin in boiling water; stir in lemon juice. Drain syrup from raspberries and add to gelatin mixture; beat in mayonnaise. Chill, stirring several times until slightly thickened. Stir in whipped topping; fold in marshmallows and raspberries. Spoon into an 8-cup mold and chill several hours or until firm.

* * *

FROZEN CREAM WITH RASPBERRIES

1 (8 oz.) pkg. cream
    cheese, softened
1 c. confectioners' sugar

1 c. light cream
½ tsp. vanilla
2 c. fresh raspberries

Beat softened cream cheese until very smooth. Gradually add confectioners' sugar, cream and vanilla. Beat until well blended. It will be quite thin. Pour into paper-lined muffin tins and freeze about 2 hours or until firm. Peel off paper, place on serving dishes, allow to soften slightly and spoon fruit around each dessert. Makes 8 to 10 servings.

Rich and easy delightful summer dessert!

* * *

RASPBERRY ICE CREAM CAKE

1 sm. frozen pound cake,
    thawed
1 sm. pkg. pistachio instant
    pudding mix*
1 c. cold milk
1 pt. vanilla ice cream,
    softened
1 (12 oz.) container frozen
    whipped topping

1 pt. raspberries,
    washed and drained
1/8 tsp. almond extract
2 Tbls. sugar
2 tsp. cornstarch
$\frac{1}{2}$ c. water
3 drops red
    food coloring

Cut about half the cake into 12 thin slices. Use remaining cake for another dessert. Combine pudding mix and milk in bowl and beat 1 minute. Add ice cream and beat 1 minute longer. Measure 1 cup of whipped topping and set aside. Add extract to remaining whipped topping; fold into pudding mixture, blending well. Spoon about $\frac{1}{4}$ of the pudding mixture into 9x5-inch loaf pan and spread evenly. Arrange 4 of the cake slices on filling; top with another $\frac{1}{4}$ of the filling. Repeat layers, ending with filling. Freeze until firm.

Meanwhile, combine sugar and cornstarch in small saucepan; add water. Cook and stir over medium heat until mixture comes to a boil. Cool; then add food coloring and pour over raspberries in bowl. Unmold ice cream cake onto platter; garnish with reserved whipped topping and some of the raspberries. Cut into slices and serve with remaining raspberries.

*Chocolate instant pudding mix may be substituted for pistachio.

* * *

FROSTY RASPBERRY SQUARES

1 c. flour
$\frac{1}{4}$ c. brown sugar
$\frac{1}{2}$ c. walnuts, chopped
$\frac{1}{2}$ c. margarine, melted
$\frac{1}{4}$ tsp. salt
2 egg whites

2/3 c. sugar
2 c. raspberries, washed
    and drained
1 Tbl. lemon juice
1 c. whipping cream,
    whipped

Combine first 5 ingredients and spread on bottom of 9x13-inch baking pan. Bake at 350° for 20 minutes, stirring occasionally. Remove half of crumbs (for topping) and spread remaining crumbs out evenly. Beat egg whites until soft peaks are formed. Gradually add sugar and beat until stiff peaks are formed. Fold in raspberries and lemon juice. Combine raspberry mixture, whipped cream and reserved crumbs, mixing gently; spoon over crumbs. Freeze 6 hours or overnight.

RASPBERRY-CHOCOLATE FROST

1 pt. chocolate ice cream,   1 (10 oz.) pkg. frozen
  softened   raspberries,
4 c. milk   thawed

In a large mixing bowl, beat ice cream and raspberries, adding milk gradually. Serve in chilled glasses. Makes about 6 (1 cup) servings.

* * *

RASPBERRY YOGURT SHAKE

1 c. plain or raspberry yogurt $\frac{1}{4}$ c. honey
$\frac{1}{2}$ c. milk   1 c. raspberries

Blend in blender for 2 minutes and enjoy!

* * *

RED BERRY SPARKLE

$\frac{1}{2}$ c. sugar   1 (10 oz.) pkg. frozen
1 (.24 oz. or .15 oz.) pkg.   raspberries in syrup,
  raspberry flavor un-   partially thawed
  sweetened soft drink mix   1 (32 oz.) bottle lemon-
4 c. cold water   lime carbonated
$\frac{1}{2}$ c. ReaLime Reconstituted   beverage, chilled
  Lime Juice   Ice

In small punch bowl or large pitcher, stir together sugar and drink mix; add water, stirring until sugar dissolves. Add ReaLime and raspberries. Just before serving, add carbonated beverage and ice.

Reprinted permission of ReaLemon/ReaLime Products.

* * *

RED RASPBERRY VINEGAR

2 qts. red raspberries   2 lbs. sugar
               1 qt. cider vinegar

Mix raspberries and vinegar. Let stand in a crock or a porcelain pan overnight. The next day, strain and add sugar. Boil 20 minutes. Seal in sterilized pint jars. To serve, dilute with ice water to make a drink, or serve as is over ice cream.

RASPBERRY FREEZER JAM

4 c. raspberries   1 tsp. butter or margarine
4 c. sugar   ½ tsp. alum

Mash berries, one layer at a time, and bring to a rolling
boil, boiling hard for 1 minute. Remove from heat and
add alum and butter. Beat with rotary or hand mixer for
5 minutes. Ladle quickly into scalded containers. Cover
at once with tight lids. Let stand at room temperature
24 hours; then store in freezer.

* * *

POTPOURRI JAM

2 qts. raspberries   2 Tbls. lemon   juice
1 qt. blueberries,   1 tsp. Fruit Fresh
   crushed   2 (1 3/4 oz.) pkg.
5½ c. sugar   powdered pectin
½ tsp. ground cinnamon   1 c. water

In medium saucepan, combine raspberries, blueberries,
sugar, cinnamon, lemon juice and Fruit Fresh. Allow to
stand 20 minutes. Bring berry mixture to a boil long
enough to dissolve sugar. The berry mixture will become
transparent when sugar dissolves.

In a small saucepan, combine pectin and water. Bring
to a boil for 1 minute; stirring constantly. Pour hot
pectin into berry mixture, stirring constantly for 2 minutes. Ladle quickly into freezer jars or containers.
Let stand at room temperature until fruit has set (approximately 24 hours). Store in freezer.

Use only tight fitting lids and remember to wash, scald
and drain both the containers and lids!

* * *

55

RASPBERRY CRESCENTS

1 c. flour
1 sm. pkg. cream cheese,
   softened
          ½ c. butter or
            margarine, softened
          ¼ c. raspberry preserves
      Confectioners' Sugar Frosting*

Combine flour, cream cheese and butter and knead with hands to form dough. Divide dough in half and shape each in a ball. Wrap and chill. On lightly floured surface, roll out each ball to about a 9-inch circle and cut into 12 wedges. Put ½ teaspoon raspberry preserves on wide end of wedge and roll toward point. Place point down on greased cookie sheet, shaping it into a crescent and bake 10 to 15 minutes at 400°. Cool and drizzle with Confectioners' Sugar Frosting.

*Confectioners' Sugar Frosting: Combine ½ cup confectioners' sugar and 2 teaspoons lemon juice. Mix until blended.

Makes 2 dozen cookie crescents.

* * *

BAMA-MERINGUE BARS

3/4 c. butter or
   margarine, softened
3/4 c. sugar
2 eggs, separated
1½ c. unsifted flour
      1 Tbl. milk
      1 c. chopped nuts
      3/4 c. Bama Red Raspberry Or Blackberry Preserves

Preheat oven to 350°. In large mixer bowl, cream butter and ¼ cup sugar until fluffy. Beat in egg yolks. Stir in flour and milk. Spread evenly in ungreased 9x13-inch baking pan. Bake 15 to 18 minutes.

Meanwhile, beat egg whites until soft peaks form, gradually add remaining ½ cup sugar, beating until stiff peaks form. Fold in nuts. Bake 25 minutes longer or until meringue is lightly browned. Cool completely. Cut into bars. Makes 2 dozen bars.

Reprinted permission of Bama Products.

* * *

CHOCOLATE RASPBERRY PIE

1 sm. pkg. regular choco-
   late pudding mix
2 (10 oz.) pkgs. frozen
   raspberries, thawed

½ c. milk
1 8-inch graham
   cracker crust
Whipped cream for topping

Combine chocolate pudding mix, undrained thawed raspberries
and milk. Bring to a boil, stirring constantly. Pour
into pie crust and chill until ready to serve. Top with
whipped cream, if desired.

* * *

RASPBERRY YOGURT PIE

2 (8 oz.) containers
   raspberry yogurt
½ c. mashed raspberries
       1 9-inch graham cracker crust

1 (8 oz.) carton frozen
   whipped topping,
   thawed

Fold yogurt and fruit into whipped topping, blending well.
Spoon into crust and freeze until firm. Place in refrigerator 30 minutes before cutting. Store leftover pie in
freezer.

* * *

FRESH APRICOT MELBA PIE

1 9-in. baked pie shell
1 qt. vanilla ice
   cream, softened
1 (10 oz.) pkg. frozen
   raspberries

2 tsp. cornstarch
2 Tbls. sugar
15 fresh California
   apricots, well
   chilled

Fill pie shell with ice cream; freeze at least 1 hour.

Meanwhile, prepare melba sauce. Place raspberries in
colander over bowl; allow to thaw at room temperature
for about 30 minutes or until 1/3 cup raspberry syrup
has dripped into bowl. Blend cornstarch and sugar in
small saucepan; stir in raspberry syrup gradually. Bring
mixture to a boil; simmer just until thickened and clear.
Cool mixture, then stir in raspberries. If necessary,
chill melba sauce until needed.

At serving time, halve and pit apricots and arrange in
attractive pattern over top of pie. Spoon melba sauce
on top and serve immediately.

* * *

FRESH NO-BAKE RASPBERRY PIE

4 c. fresh raspberries
½ c. plus 1/3 c. water
1 c. sugar

3 Tbls. cornstarch
1 baked 9-in. pie shell
Whipped or ice cream

Combine 1 cup raspberries and ½ cup water and cook for 3 minutes. Combine the sugar, cornstarch and remaining water in a small saucepan and cook until thick and clear. Add to first mixture, stirring gently. Put 3 cups fresh raspberries into cooled pie shell, pour cooked berry mixture over fresh berries and chill. Serve with whipped cream or ice cream, if desired.

Dorothy Srock

* * *

RASPBERRY ICE CREAM PIE

1 (6 oz.) pkg. raspberry
   gelatin
1¼ c. boiling water
1 pt. vanilla ice cream

1 c. fresh raspberries
1 baked 9-inch pie
   shell
Whipped cream for garnish

Dissolve gelatin in boiling water; stir in ice cream until melted. Chill until mixture starts to thicken. Fold in fruit. Pour into pie shell and chill until firm. Top with whipped cream, if desired.

* * *

RASPBERRY QUICK 'N LIGHT PIE

1 9-in. baked graham
   cracker crumb crust
1 (3 oz.) pkg. raspberry
   gelatin
2/3 c. boiling water

3½ c. frozen whipped
   topping, thawed
1 c. fresh raspberries,
   washed and drained
2 c. ice cubes

Completely dissolve gelatin in boiling water; add ice cubes and stir constantly until gelatin is thickened. Remove any unmelted ice and blend in whipped topping, whipping until smooth. Fold in raspberries. Spoon into pie crust and chill until set.

Judy Tulgren

* * *

QUICK RASPBERRY DESSERT

1 (3 oz.) pkg. raspberry
  gelatin
1¼ c. boiling water

1 pint vanilla
  ice cream
½ c. whole raspberries

Wash and drain raspberries. Combine gelatin and boiling water and blend until gelatin is dissolved. Add ice cream and blend again until smooth; chill until partially thickened. Fold in raspberries and pour into 4 dessert cups. Chill until set. Serve with a dollop of whipped cream.

* * *

EASY RASPBERRY-MARSHMALLOW DESSERT

3 c. miniature marshmallows
1 pint whipping cream,
  whipped

1 c. fresh raspberries,
  washed and drained
1 c. chopped pecans

Stir marshmallows into whipped cream. Fold in well-drained raspberries. Spoon into dessert cups and refrigerate. Before serving, sprinkle with chopped nuts.

* * *

RASPBERRY PUDDING

1 (10 oz.) pkg. frozen raspberries, thawed and
  drained (reserve liquid)
Water

1 sm. box vanilla pudding
  mix (NOT instant)
½ c. whipping cream,
  whipped

To the reserved raspberry syrup, add enough water to equal 1½ cups. In a small saucepan, combine vanilla pudding and liquid and cook according to package directions. Chill; fold in whipped cream and spoon into individual custard cups. Top with raspberries.

* * *

KID'S RASPBERRY DESSERT

1 (10 oz.) pkg. frozen raspberries, partially thawed

2 c. rice cereal
1 c. whipping cream, whipped

Just before serving, layer cereal, berries, and whipped cream in glass serving dishes, being sure to use the raspberry syrup along with the raspberries. End with whipped cream and a few berries on top. Makes about 6 desserts.

* * *

PEACHES MELBA was first made by George Auguste Escoffier, considered by many the greatest chef in history. As a tribute to the Australian opera soprano, Dame Nellie Melba, Escoffier sculpted a swan in ice and placed a bowl of vanilla ice cream between its wings. As a topping, he used peaches that had been soaked in vanilla syrup and covered with a pureé of fresh raspberries.

Make your tribute as follows:

PEACHES MELBA

1 pint Louis Sherry Vanilla
   Ice Cream
4 fresh peach halves

Melba Sauce*
Whipped cream for top-
   ping, if desired

On a dessert plate or in a stemmed dessert glass, place a slice or scoop of ice cream. Top with a peach half, cut side down. Spoon Melba Sauce over peaches. Top with whipped cream, if desired. Makes 4 servings.

MELBA SAUCE: Combine 1 (10 oz.) package frozen raspber-ries, thawed and ½ cup currant jelly in a saucepan and bring to a boil over medium heat. Mix 1½ teaspoons corn-starch and 1 tablespoon water. Add to raspberry mixture and stir constantly until thickened. Strain and chill. Makes 1 cup.

Reprinted permission of Louis Sherry Ice Cream Company.

* * *

APRICOT MELBAS

1 (10 oz.) pkg. frozen raspberries, thawed
2 tsp. cornstarch
1 Tbl. water

½ c. red currant jelly
2 pts. vanilla ice cream
1 can (17 oz.) apricot
   halves, chilled,
   and drained

MELBA SAUCE: In electric blender container, pureé rasp-berries until smooth. Strain; discard seeds. In small saucepan, mix cornstarch and water. Stir in raspberry pureé and jelly. Cook, stirring constantly, until sauce thickens and boils 1 minute. Cool, then chill.

TO SERVE: Into 6 individual dessert dishes, place a scoop of ice cream. Add 2 apricot halves to each and top with about 2 or 3 tablespoons Melba Sauce. Serve immediately. Store in refrigerator up to 1 week.

Reprinted permission of California Apricot Advisory Board.

* * *

PEACHES CARDINAL
(Poached Peaches with Raspberry Puree)
Serves 8

6 c. water	1 four-inch piece of
2 c. sugar	vanilla bean OR 3
8 large ripe but firm peaches,	tablespoons vanilla
peeled, halved and stoned	extract

In a heavy 3 or 4 quart saucepan, bring the water and sugar to a boil over high heat, stirring until sugar dissolves. Boil this syrup briskly for 3 minutes, then reduce heat as low as possible. Add peeled peach halves and vanilla and poach them uncovered at a very low simmer for 10 to 20 minutes, or until they are barely tender when pierced with the tip of a sharp knife. Refrigerate peaches in syrup until they are cold.

SAUCE CARDINAL: With the back of a large spoon, pureé 2 (10 oz.) packages frozen raspberries, defrosted and thoroughly drained, through a fine sieve into a small mixing bowl. Stir 2 tablespoons granulated sugar and 1 tablespoon Kirsch, if desired, into the raspberry pureé. Refrigerate, tightly covered.

CREME CHANTILLY: With a wire whisk, rotary or electric beater, whip 3/4 cup thoroughly chilled heavy cream in a chilled mixing bowl until it begins to thicken. Sprinkle in 2 tablespoons of sugar and 1 tablespoon vanilla extract; continue beating until the cream is firm enough to hold soft peaks on the beater when it is raised out of the bowl.

TO SERVE: Transfer chilled peach halves with a slotted spoon to individual dessert dishes or arrange them attractively on a large platter. If you wish, you can place the halves on top of one another to resemble whole peaches. (Discard the syrup or save it to use for poaching fruit again.) Mask each of the peaches thoroughly with Sauce Cardinal. Decorate with the Creme Chantilly. Garnish with whole raspberries, if desired.

* * *

RASPBERRY-PEACH QUICKIE

Melt remnants of raspberry jelly and flavor with Kirsch. Pour over peach halves and sprinkle with crushed nuts or coconut.

* * *

61

RASPBERRY TRIFLE I

6 c. pound cake cubes
(1 lb. loaf cake)
1 (4 3/4 oz.) pkg. vanilla
pudding and pie filling
mix, prepared according
to package directions
2 lg. bananas, sliced OR

1 (16 oz.) can peach
slices, well drained
ReaLemon Reconstituted
Lemon Juice
$\frac{1}{4}$ to $\frac{1}{2}$ c. cream sherry
1 c. Bama Red Raspberry
Preserves

Dip bananas in ReaLemon; set aside. In large bowl, layer half the cake cubes, sherry, preserves, fruit and pudding. Repeat layering. Chill thoroughly before serving. Refrigerate leftovers.

Reprinted permission of ReaLemon/ReaLime Products and Bama Products.

* * *

RASPBERRY TRIFLE II

1 (2-layer) white or
yellow cake mix
3 c. fresh raspberries,
washed and
drained

1 lg. pkg. vanilla
pudding mix
1 pt. whipping cream,
whipped
1 c. slivered almonds

Make cake mix in 2 8-inch round pans. Slice each cake in half, making 4 thin 8-inch rounds (a thread works well to slice the cakes). Prepare vanilla pudding mix according to package directions. Put 1 cake round on a plate and add $\frac{1}{4}$ of the pudding, spreading evenly over cake, sprinkle with 3/4 cup raspberries, $\frac{1}{4}$ of the whipped cream and $\frac{1}{4}$ cup slivered almonds. Repeat 3 more times. Refrigerate.

* * *

DREAMY CAKE

1 qt. vanilla ice cream
1 can (17 oz.) apricot halves,
sliced and drained

1 pkg. (10 oz.) frozen
raspberries, thawed
2 c. small marshmallows

Soften vanilla ice cream. Beat in apricots and raspberries. Fold in marshmallows. Pour into container, cover and place near coils in freezer. Freeze until hard. Serve "as is" or with fudge sauce or whipped cream.

Reprinted permission of California Apricot Advisory Board.

* * *

RASPBERRY MERINGUE TORTE

1 c. butter or margarine,
   softened
½ c. sugar
5 egg yolks
2 c. unsifted flour
½ tsp. baking powder
½ tsp. salt

2 Tbls. milk
1 tsp. vanilla extract
1 (16 oz.) jar Bama
   Red Raspberry Preserves
Meringue*
2 c. (1 pt.) sour cream
1 c. flaked coconut

Preheat oven to 350°. In large mixer bowl, cream butter and sugar. Add egg yolks; beat well. Sift or stir together flour, baking powder and salt; add to creamed mixture along with milk and vanilla. Mix well (batter will be stiff). Spread equal portions evenly in 4 greased 8-inch round cake pans. Spread 1/3 cup preserves over each layer.

Prepare meringue. Spread equal portions evenly over each layer. Bake 25 to 30 minutes or until lightly browned. Cool 15 minutes; remove from pans and cool completely.

Combine sour cream and coconut. Spread on 3 meringue layers; stack layers, topping with remaining layer. Chill thoroughly before serving. Makes 12 to 14 servings.

*MERINGUE: In small mixer bowl, beat 5 egg whites, 1 teaspoon vanilla and ¼ teaspoon salt until soft peaks form. Gradually add 1 cup sugar and continue beating until stiff peaks form.

Reprinted permission of Bama Products.

* * *

FROZEN RASPBERRY CREAM CHEESECAKE

1 c. graham crackers
3 Tbls. sugar
½ tsp. cinnamon
3 Tbls. butter or
   margarine, melted

2 (8 oz.) pkgs. cream
   cheese, softened
1 qt. vanilla ice cream
3/4 c. raspberry preserves
½ c. whipping cream, whipped

Combine crumbs, sugar, cinnamon and butter in small bowl and blend well. Press firmly over bottom and sides of 8 or 9-inch springform pan; chill. Beat cream cheese until soft and add softened ice cream beating just until blended. Spoon about ¼ of this mixture into prepared pan; drizzle part of raspberry preserves over; repeating until all of cheese mixture and preserves are used. Cover with plastic wrap and freeze overnight or until firm. Remove cake from freezer about ½ hour before serving and spread ¼ cup of raspberry preserves over top. Serve topped with whipped cream.

RASPBERRY BARS

½ c. butter or
  margarine, softened
1½ c. flour
½ tsp. baking soda
1 tsp. lemon juice

1 c. brown sugar
½ tsp. salt
1½ c. quick cooking
  oats
2/3 c. raspberry jam

Cream butter and sugar; stir together flour, salt and soda; add to creamed mixture. Add oats and ¼ cup water;mix until crumbly. Firmly pat half the mixture into greased 9x13-inch baking pan. Stir lemon juice into jam; spread over base. Sprinkle with remaining crumb mixture. Bake at 350° for 25 minutes.

* * *

RASPBERRY FILLED COOKIES

1 c. butter or
  margarine, softened
1 sm. pkg. instant
  chocolate pudding
1 egg
2 c. flour

3 Tbls. sugar
½ c. raspberry jam
½ c. semi-sweet
  chocolate chips
3 Tbls. margarine,
  melted

Heat oven to 325°. In a large bowl, cream margarine and pudding mix until light and fluffy; beat in egg. Gradually add flour at low speed until well mixed. Shape into 1-inch balls and roll in sugar. Place 2 inches apart on ungreased cookie sheet. With thumb, make imprint in center of each cookie. Bake for 15 to 18 minutes or until firm to touch. Remove immediately; cool.

Fill each imprint with ½ teaspoon jam. In small saucepan, blend chocolate chips and margarine over low heat until chocolate melts, stirring constantly. Drizzle ½ teaspoon over each cookie. Makes about 48 cookies.

* * *

RASPBERRY MOUSSE

1 c. sour cream
1 (10 oz.) pkg. frozen
   raspberries, thawed

1 c. sugar
1 Tbl. lemon juice
Whipped cream for garnish

Combine all ingredients in blender; blend until smooth. Pour into loaf pan; freeze. To serve, scoop out with ice cream scooper into sherbet dishes. Garnish with whipped cream and a few raspberries, if desired.

* * *

POACHED PEARS WITH RASPBERRY SAUCE

1 c. sugar
Juice of 1 lemon
2 c. water

6 fresh pears
1 (10 oz.) pkg. frozen
   raspberries, thawed

Combine sugar, 2 cups water and lemon juice in a large pan. Cover and bring to a boil. In the meantime, peel pears, removing end cores but leaving on stems and place in boiling syrup; cover and simmer until tender; chill. Place package of thawed raspberries in blender and whirl until blended; strain to remove seeds. Serve over pears.

* * *

LEMON-SOUR CREAM TARTS

1 can lemon pudding OR
   2 c. canned pie filling
1 c. dairy sour cream
10 baked tart shells

1 (10 oz.) pkg. frozen
   raspberries, thawed
2 Tbls. sugar
1 Tbl. cornstarch

Stir together pudding and sour cream; chill. Drain raspberries, reserving 2/3 cup syrup. Mix sugar and cornstarch in small saucepan; gradually stir in reserved syrup. Cook and stir until mixture thickens and boils; remove from heat and chill. Fill tart shells with lemon mixture; top with a few raspberries and spoon about 1 tablespoon raspberry glaze over each tart.

* * *

RASPBERRY MACAROON MOUSSE

2 pkg. (16 oz. ea.) frozen
   raspberries, thawed
2 c. heavy cream

2 egg whites
$\frac{1}{2}$ c. sugar
24 small coconut cookies

Assemble Blender. Put raspberries and syrup into blender container. Cover and process at Pureé. Strain and pour into large mixer bowl. Assemble Mixer. Beat egg whites in small mixer bowl until frothy. Gradually add sugar and continue beating until stiff but not dry. Fold into puréed raspberries.

Whip cream in small mixer bowl and fold into raspberry mixture. Pour into a 2-quart mold and place in freezer for 1 hour.

Meanwhile, break half the coconut cookies into blender container, cover and process 3 cycles at Grind. Empty onto waxed paper and repeat with remaining cookies. Cover partially frozen mousse with crumbs, swirl with a knife to form streaks. Return to freezer and freeze until firm, 3 or 4 hours. Yield: 6-8 servings.

Reprinted Courtesy Oster.

* * *

OLD-FASHIONED STREUSEL COFFEE CAKE

3 c. flour
1 c. sugar
1 tsp. baking powder
1 tsp. baking soda
$\frac{1}{2}$ tsp. salt
1 c. butter or margarine
$\frac{1}{2}$ c. chopped nuts

2 Tbls. light brown sugar
1 Tbl. apple pie spice
2 eggs
1 c. buttermilk or sour milk
1 tsp. pure vanilla extract
4 Tbls. raspberry
   preserves, divided

In a large mixing bowl, sift flour, sugar, baking powder, baking soda and salt. Cut in butter with a pastry blender or 2 knives until mixture resembles coarse crumbs. Remove $\frac{1}{2}$ cup crumb mixture. Into it stir nuts, brown sugar and apple pie spice; set aside. Add eggs, buttermilk and vanilla extract to unspiced mixture, blending until smooth. Spread 1/3 of the batter in a buttered 9-inch tube pan. Spoon 2 tablespoons of the preserves in center of batter; sprinkle with 1/3 crumb mixture. Repeat, layering batter, preserves and crumb mixture two more times, omitting preserves on top layer. Bake in a preheated moderate oven (350°) 45 to 50 minutes or until a cake tester inserted into center comes out clean. Cool in a pan on a rack for 10 minutes. Remove from pan and serve warm or cool.

STRAWBERRIES

FRESH STRAWBERRY PIE I

1 baked 9-in. pie shell
1 qt. fresh strawberries
½ c. confectioners' sugar

1 c. water
½ to 3/4 c. sugar
2½ Tbls. cornstarch

Wash and cut berries. Mix 3 cups of the berries with the confectioners' sugar. Let stand 1 hour. Cook remaining berries with water until tender. Rub through strainer. Return to heat. Mix sugar and cornstarch and add to strawberry juice. Cook over medium heat until clear. Place uncooked berries in pie shell, pour hot glaze over; let cool and then refrigerate.

* * *

FRESH STRAWBERRY PIE II

1½ c. sugar
4 Tbls. cornstarch
1 pint fresh strawberries,
   sliced

½ c. water
4 Tbls. strawberry gelatin
1 baked 9-in. pie shell
Whipped cream for garnish

Cook sugar, cornstarch, water and gelatin until slightly thickened. Remove from heat and add fresh strawberries. Pour into baked pie shell. Serve topped with whipped cream and a few whole strawberries, if desired.

* * *

STRAWBERRY VANILLA PUDDING PIES

2 baked 9-in. pie shells
1 lg. pkg. vanilla pudding mix
3 (10 oz.) pkgs. frozen
   strawberries

6 Tbls. cornstarch
1/8 tsp. lemon juice
Whipped cream for garnish

Cook pudding according to package directions. Pour half into each pie shell. Let cool. Put strawberries in a large saucepan and add cornstarch. Cook until thick; 5 to 10 minutes. Add lemon juice; let cool. Pour over pudding in shells. Chill. Serve, topped with whipped cream.

* * *

STRAWBERRY GLAZE PIE I

1 baked 9-in. pie shell	1/3 c. water
1 qt. fresh strawberries	2½ Tbls. cornstarch
1 c. sugar	Whipped cream for garnish

Line shell with whole berries, reserving 1 cup for the glaze. Crush reserved berries and add 3/4 cup sugar and water. Cook slightly. Mix remaining ¼ cup sugar with cornstarch and add to first mixture; continue cooking until thick. Cool slightly and pour over berries in shell. Chill; top with whipped cream.

* * *

STRAWBERRY GLAZE PIES II

2 baked 9-in. pie shells	1 c. water
6 c. fresh strawberries	2 Tbls. lemon juice
2 c. sugar	Whipped cream for
6 Tbls. cornstarch	garnish

Crush enough washed and hulled berries to make 2 cups and combine with sugar and cornstarch in a medium saucepan. Add water and cook, stirring constantly until thickened. Stir in lemon juice, cover and cool to lukewarm. Place remaining berries, whole or sliced, in each pie shell. Pour glaze ove berries and chill. Serve, topped with whipped cream.

Note: These pies must be eaten the same day as the crust gets soggy.

Dorothy Srock

* * *

BERRIED-TREASURE PIE

1 (8 oz.) pkg. cream cheese, softened	1 c. strawberries, halved
2 Tbls. sugar	1 envelope packaged whipped topping, prepared
2 Tbls. milk	1 sm. pkg. lemon instant pudding mix
1 baked 9-in. graham cracker crust	1 c. milk

Beat softened cream cheese with sugar and 2 tablespoons milk in a bowl until smooth. Spread evenly in pie crust. Arrange strawberries on cream cheese mixture. Prepare pudding mix with 1 cup milk; fold in whipped topping. Spoon onto pie. Chill at least 2 hours.

Judy Tulgren

MICHIGAN GLAZED STRAWBERRY PIE

1 baked 9-in. pie shell
1 qt. drained, hulled,
   Michigan strawberries
1½ c. strawberry juice

1 (3 oz.) pkg. cream
   cheese, softened
1 c. sugar
3 Tbls. cornstarch

Spread softened cream cheese over bottom of pastry shell. Cover with half of the berries (choicest). Mash and strain rest of berries until juice is extracted; add water, if necessary, to make 1½ cups juice. Bring juice to boil; stir in sugar and cornstarch. Cook over low heat, stirring constantly, until boiling. Boil 1 minute. Pour over berries in pie shell. Chill 2 hours. Just before serving, decorate with whipped cream.

* * *

MICHIGAN TRIPLE FRUIT PIE

1 pkg. (3 oz.) strawberry OR
   mixed fruit flavor gelatin
2/3 c. boiling water
2 c. ice cubes
2 Tbls. brandy
1 Tbl. orange liqueur

1 carton (8 oz.) frozen
   whipped topping, thawed
½ c. strawberries, sliced
½ c. peaches, sliced
½ c. blueberries
1 baked 9-in. pie shell

Dissolve gelatin completely in boiling water, stirring about 3 minutes. Add ice cubes and stir constantly until gelatin is thickened, about 2 to 3 minutes. Remove any unmelted ice. Fold brandy and liqueur into whipped topping. Blend whipped topping mixture into gelatin, whipping until smooth. Fold in Michigan strawberries, peaches, and blueberries. Chill if necessary, until mixture will mound. Spoon into cooled pie shell. Chill. Garnish with additional whipped topping and fresh Michigan fruits, if desired.

* * *

QUICK 'N' EASY DESSERT

Combine banana slices, fresh strawberries, and green grapes into dessert dishes. Top with orange sherbet.

* * *

FRESH DOUBLE STRAWBERRY PIES

2 baked 9-in. pie shells
2 qts. fresh strawberries;
    washed, hulled, sliced
1½ c. sugar

2 c. hot water
4 Tbls. cornstarch
1 (3 oz.) pkg. straw-
    berry gelatin

Dissolve gelatin in hot water and add to sugar and cornstarch. Mix well and cook until cornstarch is clear and
thickened slightly. Place strawberries equally in both
crusts and pour sauce evenly over both. Liquid will thick-
en as pie cools. Ice cream or whipped cream makes an
excellent garnish!

* * *

BIG STRAWBERRY TART

3 pts. fresh strawberries
2½ Tbls. cornstarch
2 drops red food coloring

3/4 c. sugar
½ c. water
1 baked 9-in. pie shell

Wash and hull strawberries. Crush 1 pint of the berries.
In a saucepan, blend together sugar, cornstarch and water.
Add the crushed berries and food coloring. Bring to a
boil and cook until mixture is clear; about 2 minutes.
Strain. Arrange remaining whole berries in baked pie
shell. Spoon glaze over berries, carefully coating each
berry. Cool.

* * *

STRAWBERRY ROMANOFF PIE

1 sm. pkg. vanilla
    pudding mix
1 (3 oz.) pkg. straw-
    berry gelatin
2 c. water
3 Tbls. orange juice

1 (8 oz.) carton frozen
    whipped topping
1 pint strawberries,
    hulled
1 baked 9-inch
    pie shell

Combine pudding mix, gelatin and water in saucepan. Cook
and stir over medium heat until mixture comes to a boil.
Add orange juice and chill until thickened. Beat in 2
cups whipped topping. Arrange whole strawberries, with
pointed ends up, in pie shell, reserving several for garnish, if desired. Top with filling; chill about 2 hours.
Garnish with remaining whipped topping and reserved strawberries.

* * *

FRENCH STRAWBERRY PIE

1 baked 9-in. pie shell
1 (3 oz.) pkg. cream cheese
3 Tbls. fresh OR
   soured cream
1 quart fresh straw-
   berries, cleaned

1 c. sugar
3 Tbls. cornstarch
1 Tbl. lemon juice plus
   enough water to
   equal $\frac{1}{2}$ cup
Whipped cream for garnish

Blend together cream cheese and cream until smooth. Spread over bottom of pie shell. Mash enough strawberries to measure 1 cup. Mix sugar and cornstarch in saucepan; stir in lemon juice, water and strawberries. Cook over medium heat, stirring constantly, until mixture thickens and boils. Boil 1 minute longer stirring constantly. Cool slightly. Arrange remaining berries, stem end down, over cream cheese mixture in pie plate. If berries are very large, you may want to halve them. Pour cooked straw- berry mixture over top. Refrigerate until set, at least 3 hours. Serve, topped with whipped cream.

* * *

STRAWBERRY PUDDING PIE

1 baked 9-in. pie shell
$\frac{1}{2}$ c. sugar
1 Tbl. cornstarch
2 eggs
2 c. hot milk

1 tsp. vanilla
1 qt. fresh strawberries,
   cleaned and halved
Whipped cream for
   garnish

Combine sugar, cornstarch and eggs. Add to hot milk and cook together until thick. Add vanilla. Cool. Pour into pie shell. Smooth over and arrange sliced berries on top of pudding, starting with the pointed ends of ber- ries toward the crust going around the crust. Then lay another circle of berries until pudding is completely covered. Sprinkle lightly with sugar. Serve, topped with whipped cream.

* * *

STRAWBERRY PARFAIT PIE

1 baked 9-in. pie shell
1 (3 oz.) pkg. lemon gelatin
$1\frac{1}{4}$ c. hot water

2 c. strawberry ice cream
$1\frac{1}{2}$ c. fresh strawberries,
   washed, hulled, sliced

Dissolve gelatin in hot water in a 2-quart saucepan. Add ice cream, stirring until melted. Chill until slightly thickened; about 15 minutes. Fold in drained strawberries and turn into cooled pie shell. Chill until firm.

EASY STRAWBERRY CHEESE PIE

1 (8 oz.) pkg. cream
  cheese, softened
¼ c. sugar
1 c. whipping cream, whipped

1½ c. fresh straw-
  berries, sliced
1 baked 9-in. graham
  cracker pie shell

Beat softened cream cheese and sugar together until thoroughly blended. Fold in whipped cream; then sliced strawberries. Spoon into pie shell and chill thoroughly; at least 2 hours.

* * *

STRAWBERRY CHIFFON PIE

1 Tbl. unflavored gelatin
½ c. boiling water
¼ tsp. salt
2 egg whites, stiffly beaten
1 c. whipping cream, whipped
¼ c. cold water

3/4 c. sugar
1 c. mashed strawberries
¼ c. sugar
1 baked 9-in. pie shell
Whipped cream for topping
Whole strawberries for garnish

Soak gelatin in cold water. Add boiling water, 3/4 cup sugar and mashed strawberries. Let cool until partially stiffened. Fold in egg whites, ¼ cup sugar plus the whipped cream. Let stand in cool pie shell until set. Garnish with whipped cream and whole strawberries, as desired.

* * *

STRAWBERRY SUNDAE PIE

1 9-in. baked pie shell
3 egg whites (use only Grade
  A clean, uncracked eggs)
¼ tsp. cream of tartar
6 Tbls. sugar

1 qt. strawberry or vanilla
  ice cream, slightly
  softened
1 c. Bama Strawberry
  Preserves

Preheat oven to 450°. In small mixer bowl, beat egg whites and cream of tartar until soft peaks form; gradually add sugar, beating until stiff but not dry. Set aside. Spoon half the ice cream evenly into pastry shell. Spread with preserves. Spoon remaining ice cream over top. Spread meringue on top of pie, sealing carefully to edge of shell. Bake 3 to 5 minutes or until meringue is golden brown. Freeze until firm, at least 4 hours. Remove from freezer 10 minutes before serving.

Reprinted with permission of Bama Products.

* * *

STRAWBERRY RIBBON PIE

1 (3 oz.) pkg. straw-
   berry gelatin
¼ c. sugar
1¼ c. boiling water
1 (10 oz.) pkg. frozen
   strawberries

1 c. whipped cream
1 (3 oz.) pkg. cream
   cheese, softened
1/3 c. confectioners' sugar
1 tsp. vanilla
Pinch of salt

Combine gelatin, sugar and boiling water. Add frozen strawberries and let set until starts to congeal. Mix together cream cheese, confectioners' sugar, vanilla and salt and fold whipped cream into cheese mixture. Alternate layers of berry mixture and whipped cream mixture in baked pie crust. Chill until ready to serve.

* * *

STRAWBERRY-BANANA PIE

1 (10 oz.) pkg. frozen strawberries, thawed
½ c. sugar
2 Tbls. lemon juice
2½ Tbls. cornstarch

½ c. water
1 lg. ripe banana
1 8-in. baked pie crust
Strawberry juice
Whipped cream for garnish

Mix cornstarch, sugar, water and juice from strawberries. Cook until thick and clear. Add lemon juice, mix and cool. Slice banana into baked pie shell. Add strawberries to mixture and pour over sliced banana. Chill. Serve, topped with whipped cream.

* * *

MIGHTY HIGH STRAWBERRY PIE

2 baked 9-in. pie shells
1 (10 oz.) pkg. frozen
   strawberries,
   thawed slightly
1 Tbl. lemon juice

1 c. sugar
 2 egg whites
1 c. whipping cream,
   whipped

Beat egg whites, sugar and lemon juice at high speed until fluffy. Add strawberries; fold in whipped cream. Pour into pie shells and freeze. Serve frozen. Cut with knife dipped in hot water. Refreshing summer dessert!

* * *

BLUE CHEESE CAKE

4 oz. pkg. Treasure Cave
    Blue Cheese, crumbled
2 c. graham cracker crumbs
1/3 c. melted butter OR
    margarine
2 tsp. sugar
¼ tsp. cinnamon

19 oz. (2 8 oz. pkgs. and
    1 3 oz. pkg.) cream cheese
4 eggs
1 c. sugar
4 tsp. vanilla
1 pt. dairy sour cream
2 pkgs. (10 oz. ea.) frozen
    strawberries

Blend crumbs, butter, 2 teaspoons sugar and cinnamon. Pat into bottom and sides of 9 by 3 inch springform pan. Bake 5 minutes in 425° oven. Remove; cool. Beat blue and cream cheeses until smooth. Add eggs one at a time, beating well after each addition. Gradually add 1 cup sugar. Add 2 teaspoons vanilla and whip until smooth. Pour into pan. Bake in 325° oven 1 hour. Remove and increase oven temperature to 425°. Whip sour cream with remaining vanilla. Spread over cake. Return to oven for 15 minutes. Chill. Spoon strawberries over individual servings.

Reprinted permission of Swift & Company.

* * *

RICH STRAWBERRY-RHUBARB CHEESECAKE

3 c. rhubarb, diced in
    ¼-inch pieces
2 envelopes unflavored gelatin
¼ c. plus 2 Tbls. water
2 egg yolks
1 c. sugar
1 (8 oz.) carton
    cottage cheese

1 Tbl. lemon juice
1/8 tsp. salt
2 c. strawberries; washed,
    hulled and sliced
2 egg whites, stiffly
    beaten
1 c. whipping cream,
    whipped

Combine rhubarb with ½ cup sugar and 2 tablespoons water in saucepan. Bring to a boil and simmer for 5 minutes. Drain syrup and add water to make ½ cup liquid. Soften gelatin in ¼ cup water. Mix egg yolks, ½ cup sugar and syrup. Cook until thickened. Remove from heat and add softened gelatin. Beat cottage cheese until smooth; add lemon juice and salt. Stir in egg yolk mixture. Fold in drained rhubarb and sliced strawberries. Fold in beaten egg whites and whipped cream. Pour into crust and refrigerate at least 4 hours or overnight. Use a graham cracker crust and an 8-inch springform pan.

* * *

VERY BERRY CHEESECAKE

1¼ c. graham cracker crumbs
2 Tbls. sugar
3 Tbls. butter OR
   margarine, melted
1 envelope unflavored gelatin
Water
2 (8 oz.) pkgs. cream
   cheese, softened
½ c. sugar

1½ tsp. lemon juice
1 tsp. grated lemon peel
½ tsp. vanilla extract
1 qt. strawberries,
   washed and hulled
1 pt. blueberries,
   washed and drained
2 eggs at room tempera-
   ture, separated

Stir together the graham cracker crumbs and 2 tablespoons sugar. Mix in butter thoroughly. Press mixture evenly in bottom of a 10-inch springform pan. Bake 10 minutes at 350°. Cool.

In small bowl, mix gelatin with ¼ cup cold water; let stand 5 minutes to soften. Add 3/4 cup very hot tap water to mixture and stir until gelatin is completely dissolved, about 3 minutes. In a large bowl, beat cream cheese, remaining ½ cup of sugar, egg yolks, lemon juice, lemon peel and vanilla until thoroughly mixed; gradually beat in gelatin mixture. In small bowl, beat egg whites until stiff peaks form. Fold egg whites into cheese mixture. Spoon mixture over crust in pan; cover pan with plastic wrap; refrigerate until firm. Remove side of pan from cheesecake and arrange the strawberries, pointed end up, and blueberries on top.

* * *

BERRY SPECIAL CHEESECAKE

1 c. graham cracker
   crumbs
3 Tbls. sugar
3 Tbls. butter OR
   margarine, melted

3 (8 oz.) pkgs. cream cheese
3/4 c. sugar
3 eggs
1 tsp. vanilla
2 c. strawberry jam

Combine crumbs, 3 tablespoons sugar and butter; press into bottom of a 9-inch springform pan. Bake at 325° for 10 minutes. Increase oven temperature to 450°. Combine softened cream cheese and remaining sugar, mixing at medium speed until well blended. Add eggs one at a time; add vanilla. Pour over crust and bake for 10 minutes. Reduce oven temperature to 250° and continue baking 25 to 30 minutes or until done; chill. Before serving, top with strawberry jam.

* * *

IT'S-A-SNAP CHEESECAKE

1 envelope Knox Un-
   flavored Gelatine
½ c. sugar
1 c. boiling water
2 pkgs. (8 oz. ea.) cream,
   cheese, softened

1 tsp. vanilla extract,
   optional
1/3 c. strawberry
   preserves
1 9-inch graham
   cracker crust

In large bowl, mix unflavored gelatine with sugar; add boiling water and stir until gelatine is completely dissolved. With electric mixer, beat in cream cheese and vanilla until smooth. Pour into prepared crust and chill 10 minutes; then swirl in strawberry preserves. Chill until firm.

Reprinted permission of Knox Gelatine, Inc.

* * *

JEWELLED MINI CHEESECAKES

1½ c. graham cracker crumbs
6 Tbls. butter OR
   margarine, melted
½ c. plus 2 Tbls. sugar
2½ (8 oz.) pkgs. cream
   cheese, softened

4 tsp. flour
1 tsp. vanilla extract
3 eggs
Bama Strawberry Preserves
   OR any other flavor
   Bama Preserves, chilled

Preheat oven to 325°. In medium bowl, combine crumbs, butter and 2 tablespoons sugar; mix well. Spoon about 1 tablespoon mixture into ungreased muffin cups; press firmly on bottoms. In large mixer bowl, beat cheese and remaining sugar until fluffy; stir in flour and extract. Add eggs 1 at a time, beating well after each addition. Fill crumb-lined muffin cups 2/3 full. Bake 30 minutes or until toothpick inserted near center comes out clean. Cool to room temperature. Loosen cheesecakes; invert onto baking sheets. Chill. Just before serving, top with preserves. Refrigerate leftovers. Makes 2 dozen 2½-inch cheesecakes.

TIP: Cheesecakes may be made ahead, wrapped tightly and frozen, without preserve topping. Thaw completely; top with preserves to serve.

Reprinted permission of Bama Products.

* * *

STRAWBERRY SHORTCAKE

4 2/3 c. biscuit mix
1/3 c. sugar
1/3 c. margarine, melted
1 c. milk
½ c. brown sugar

2 Tbls. margarine,
  softened
1½ qts. strawberries,
  sliced
1 c. sugar
Whipped topping for garnish

Mix strawberries and 1 cup sugar and set aside. Stir biscuit mix, 1/3 cup sugar, margarine (melted) and milk to a soft dough. Knead dough on a floured board until smooth and divide in half. Put each half into an ungreased round layer pan and spread each with 1 tablespoon softened margarine and sprinkle with ¼ cup brown sugar on each. Bake 450°. Remove from pans, place one layer topside down on serving plate and spoon half the strawberry mix over shortcake. Top with other layer and remaining berries. Top with whipped topping.

* * *

STRAWBERRY SHORTCUT CAKE

1 c. miniature marshmallows
2 (10 oz.) pkgs. frozen
  strawberries, thawed
1 (3 oz.) pkg. straw-
  berry gelatin
2¼ c. flour
1½ c. sugar

½ c. shortening
1 Tbl. baking powder
½ tsp. salt
1 c. milk
1 tsp. vanilla
3 eggs
Ice or whipped cream

Grease the bottom only of a 9x13-inch pan and sprinkle marshmallows evenly over the bottom of the pan. Thoroughly combine thawed strawberries with syrup and .strawberry gelatin; set aside. Combine remaining ingredients in a large bowl and blend until moistened; beat 3 minutes. Pour batter over marshmallows and spoon strawberry mixture over batter. Bake at 350° for 45 to 50 minutes or until cake tests done. Serve warm or cold with ice cream or whipped cream.

* * *

STRAWBERRY STACK CAKE

1 pkg. refrigerator biscuits
Cooking oil

Sweetened strawberries
Whipped cream

Roll the biscuits separately on a floured surface until thin, and pierce each several times with a fork. Fry in small amount of oil until brown and crisp, turning once. Cool. Place 1 biscuit on a platter and cover with strawberries. Repeat layers until all the biscuits are used, ending with strawberries. Serve with whipped cream.

BERRY-BINGE SHORTCAKE

4 c. biscuit mix
¼ c. sugar
2 eggs
1 1/3 c. milk
2 tsp. vanilla (divided)
Grated rind of 1 orange
6 fresh apricots, pitted
   and sliced

1 pt. strawberries,
   washed, hulled, sliced
½ c. sugar
1 (3¼ oz.) pkg. vanilla
   pudding mix
2 c. milk
1 c. (½ pt.) heavy cream
¼ c. confectioners' sugar

Grease two 9-inch layer cake pans. In a bowl, combine biscuit mix, ¼ cup sugar, eggs, 1 1/3 cups milk, 1 teaspoon vanilla and orange rind. Beat until smooth and well blended. Spread mixture into prepared cake pans. Bake in a preheated 400° oven, 20 to 25 minutes or until layers are puffed and brown. Remove from pans; cool on a rack. In a bowl, mix apricots, strawberries and ½ cup sugar. In a saucepan, mix pudding with 2 cups milk; stir over low heat until pudding bubbles and thickens. Cover and chill. In a bowl, mix cream, ¼ cup confectioners' sugar and remaining 1 teaspoon vanilla; beat until stiff. Chill.

When ready to serve, place one layer on a serving plate. Spoon over one half of the fruit and its juices. Spoon pudding over fruit. Top with second layer. Spoon on remaining fruit and juices. Top with whipped cream. Chill until ready to serve.

This is a sensational dessert made up of four fabulous party layers - the life of a summer party!

* * *

RED, WHITE, AND BLUE SHORTCAKE

2 pkg. blueberry muffin mix
4 Tbls. butter or margarine
1 c. confectioners' sugar

1½ c. whipping cream, whipped
6 c. strawberries, sliced
   and sweetened

Prepare both packages of blueberry muffin mix, following package directions. Pour into 2 greased 9-inch round cake pans. Bake at 400° for 20 minutes or until cake tests done. While "shortcake" bakes, cream butter with confectioners' sugar until fluffy and smooth. Remove shortcake layers from pans; spread each with confectioners' sugar mixture; strawberries and whipped cream. Stack; cut in wedges and serve.

* * *

OLD-FASHIONED STRAWBERRY SHORTCAKE

2 c. biscuit mix
2 Tbls. sugar
¼ c. shortening
1 egg

1/3 c. whipping cream
2 Tbls. butter OR
    margarine
1 qt. fresh strawberries,
    sliced and sweetened

Combine biscuit mix and sugar. Cut in shortening. Combine egg and cream and add to first mixture. Stir with a fork until dough gathers into a soft ball. Roll out about ½-inch thick on a floured surface. Cut into individual biscuits with a 3-inch cutter and place on greased baking sheet. Dot with butter and bake for 12 to 15 minutes at 450°. Split and butter while hot. Fill and top biscuits with sweetened strawberries. Serve with whipped cream or pouring cream. Yield: 6 to 8 servings.

* * *

STRAWBERRY SHORTCAKE DELUXE

4 c. strawberries,
    sliced
1 c. milk
¼ c. confectioners'
    sugar
1¼ c. sugar

4 c. buttermilk biscuit
    mix
2 eggs
¼ c. butter OR
    margarine, softened
1 c. whipping cream,
    whipped

Combine washed, hulled and sliced strawberries and 1 cup of the sugar in a large bowl; refrigerate until ready to use. Combine biscuit mix, remaining sugar, milk, and eggs in a large bowl. Stir with a fork until blended. Spoon evenly into 2 greased 8-inch cake pans. Bake in hot oven (400°) 25 minutes or until nicely brown. Loosen around edges; turn out onto wire racks. While still warm, split each biscuit in half into two thin layers. In a small bowl, combine butter and confectioners' sugar until smooth. Spread on cut sides of cake.

Put shortcake together this way: On cut layer, spoon ¼ of the strawberries, then whipped cream; repeat with remaining layers. Garnish top with whole strawberries, if desired. Makes 6 servings.

* * *

STRAWBERRY MUFFINS

½ c. crushed, fresh
    strawberries
2 c. vanilla ice
    cream, softened

¼ c. sugar
3 c. biscuit mix
3 Tbls. Amaretto
    Liqueur

Combine crushed strawberries, sugar and Amaretto. Fold in softened ice cream. Add biscuit mix and stir just until blended. Fill paper-lined muffin cups about 2/3 full and bake in a preheated oven (375°) for about 20 minutes or until golden brown. Delicious served warm with a mixture of softened cream cheese and strawberry jam.

NOTE: These muffins also make excellent "shortcakes." Just split and top with sweetened, fresh strawberries and whipped cream.

* * *

STRAWBERRY JAM CUPCAKES

1½ c. flour
1 c. sugar
1 tsp. baking soda
1 tsp. baking powder
1 tsp. nutmeg
1 tsp. cinnamon

1 tsp. salt
½ c. shortening
1 c. buttermilk
2 eggs, beaten
1 c. strawberry jam
3/4 c. chopped nuts
    (optional)

Sift together all dry ingredients. Add shortening, buttermilk, eggs, jam and nuts. Beat together for 250 strokes. Bake in cupcake pans at 350° for 20 to 25 minutes. Makes 20 to 24 cupcakes.

* * *

STRAWBERRY DREAM CAKE

1 pkg. (2 layer) yellow
    OR white cake mix
1 envelope whipped
    topping mix

4 eggs
1 c. cold tap water
Sweetened, sliced or
    halved strawberries

Prepare whipped topping mix. Combine cake mix, whipped topping, eggs and water in large mixing bowl. Blend until moistened. Beat at medium speed for 4 minutes. Pour into greased and floured 10-inch tube pan. Bake at 350° for 45 to 50 minutes. Cool in pan 15 minutes, then remove from pan and cool on rack. Slice and serve with strawberries and prepared whipped topping.

Shelly R. Oja

* * *

80

STRAWBERRY CAKE

1 (2 layer) pkg. white
   cake mix
1 (3 oz.) pkg. straw-
   berry gelatin
$\frac{1}{2}$ c. cooking oil
Dash of salt

$\frac{1}{2}$ c. water
$\frac{1}{2}$ (10 oz.) pkg. frozen
   strawberries; mashed,
   thawed, but NOT drained
4 eggs

Place all ingredients in a bowl and mix well. Bake in greased 9x13-inch pan at 350° for 45-50 minutes. Glaze while hot with the following:

GLAZE: Melt 4 tablespoons margarine and add remaining $\frac{1}{2}$ package strawberries and scant cup of confectioners' sugar. Stir until thoroughly blended. Pour over hot cake.

* * *

STRAWBERRY GELATIN CAKE

1 pkg. (2-layer size)
   white cake mix
1 c. salad oil
3 eggs

1 pkg. (3 oz.) straw-
   berry gelatin
$\frac{1}{2}$ c. hot water
1 pkg. (10 oz.) frozen
   strawberries, thawed
   and drained

Mix all ingredients in order given (dissolve gelatin in hot water). Bake in 3 greased and floured 8 or 9-inch layer pans at 350° for 30 minutes or until cake tests done. Cool and frost with Strawberry Frosting as follows:

STRAWBERRY FROSTING: Cream $\frac{1}{2}$ cup margarine and gradually add 1 pound confectioners' sugar and 1 package (10 oz.) frozen strawberries, which have been thawed and drained. If frosting is too stiff, add some of the drained straw- berry juice.

* * *

STRAWBERRY LOAF

$1\frac{1}{2}$ c. flour
1 tsp. baking powder
1 tsp. salt
$1\frac{1}{2}$ tsp. cinnamon
1 c. sugar
2 eggs

$\frac{1}{2}$ c. chopped nuts
$\frac{1}{2}$ c. plus 2 Tbls.
   cooking oil
1 (16 oz.) pkg. frozen
   strawberries, thawed
   and drained

Mix dry ingredients; mix remaining ingredients into dry, stirring carefully but thoroughly. Pour into lightly greased 9-inch loaf pan and bake at 350° for about 1 hour. Cool in pan 10 minutes, then remove and let cool completely.

* * *

ELEGANT STRAWBERRY TORTE

3 c. sifted cake flour
½ tsp. salt
1 egg
1 tsp. baking soda
1 pint whipping
   cream, whipped

2 c. brown sugar,
   firmly packed
1 c. butter or margarine
1 c. sour milk
½ c. chopped pecans
1 pt. fresh strawberries

Mix together flour, brown sugar, salt and butter until crumbly. Reserve 1 cup crumb mixture; set aside. Combine egg, milk and baking soda. Add to remaining crumb mixture; stir well. Pour into 2 greased, paper-lined 9-inch layer pans. Sprinkle with reserved crumb mixture; then nuts. Bake at 375° for 25 to 30 minutes, or until cake tests done. Cool. Place one layer, nut side up on a serving platter. Spread with half of whipped cream. Top with sliced strawberries. Place the other layer on top. Spoon remaining whipped cream into puffs around the cake. Garnish with sliced strawberries. Serve immediately. Yield: 12 servings.

* * *

STRAWBERRY WALNUT TORTE

5 eggs, separated
1 c. confectioners' sugar
1 c. ground walnuts
7 squares unsalted soda
   crackers, crushed

2 Tbls. baking powder
1 quart strawberries,
   washed and sliced
Whipped cream

Beat egg yolks until thick and lemon colored. Gradually beat in sugar. Add nuts, crackers, and baking powder. Mixture will be very thick. Beat egg whites until stiff. Fold in beaten egg whites slowly and carefully. Bake in 3 9-inch layer cake pans at 375° for 15 minutes. Remove from pans at once. Let cool.

Spread whipped cream and strawberries in between each layer and on top. Do this about 1 hour before serving.

* * *

STRAWBERRY ANGEL DELIGHT

½ c. flour
¼ c. brown sugar
¼ c. margarine
1/3 c. chopped pecans
2 Tbls. lemon juice

1 (7 oz.) jar marsh-
   mallow creme
1 (16 oz.) pkg. frozen
   strawberries, thawed
1 c. whipping cream,
   whipped

Combine flour and sugar; cut in margarine; add nuts.
Press into 9-inch springform pan. Bake at 350° for 20
minutes; cool. Gradually add lemon juice to marshmallow
creme, mixing until well blended. Stir in strawberries,
well drained; fold in whipped cream; pour over crumb crust
and freeze. Makes 8 to 10 servings.

Shelly R. Oja

* * *

STRAWBERRY CHEESE BARS

2 c. unsifted flour
2/3 c. sugar
2 tsp. baking powder
½ tsp. salt
2 eggs

½ c. butter OR
   margarine, softened
1 (8 oz.) pkg. cream
   cheese, softened
1 c. Bama Strawberry
   Preserves

Preheat oven to 350° (325° for glass dish). In large
bowl, combine flour, sugar, baking powder, salt, butter
and 1 egg; mix until crumbly. Press half of mixture in
bottom of 13x9-inch baking pan. In small bowl, beat 1
egg and cream cheese until smooth; spread evenly over
crust. Spoon preserves over top. Sprinkle with remaining
crumb mixture; press down lightly. Bake 30 to 35 minutes
or until edges are golden brown. Cool. Cut into bars.
Store in refrigerator.

Reprinted permission of Bama Products.

STRAWBERRY NUT SQUARES

½ c. sugar
6 Tbls. butter or margarine
2 egg yolks, well beaten
1 tsp. vanilla
1½ c. flour

1 tsp. baking powder
Strawberry jam
2 egg whites
1 c. packed brown sugar
Finely chopped nuts

Blend sugar with butter. Add egg yolks, vanilla, and
flour mixed with baking powder. Mix dough well with hands.
Press in greased 9-inch square pan. Spread strawberry
jam on dough (as thick as you like). Beat egg whites
stiff. Add brown sugar and beat well. Spread over jam.
Sprinkle with nuts. Bake at 350° for 12 to 15 minutes.
Cut into squares while warm.

* * *

FRESH MICHIGAN STRAWBERRY MOUSSE

1 pint Michigan strawberries
2 pkgs. (3 oz. ea.) straw-
    berry gelatin

Water
$\frac{1}{4}$ c. sugar
1 pt. whipping cream

Crush strawberries and drain the juice; reserve. Add enough water to the juice to make 1½ cups. Bring juice to a boil and stir in gelatin; dissolve and cool. Add strawberries and sugar. Whip cream until it stands in soft peaks and fold into strawberry mixture. Pour mixture into a 2-quart mold or a 1½-quart souffle dish with a 2-inch collar. Chill several hours or overnight.

NOTE: 2 packages (10 oz. ea.) of frozen strawberries can be substituted for the fresh strawberries. Omit sugar if frozen berries are used.

* * *

STRAWBERRY SWIRL

1 c. graham cracker crumbs
$\frac{1}{4}$ c. melted butter OR
    margarine
1 c. boiling water
1 c. cold water
$\frac{1}{2}$ lb. marshmallows
$\frac{1}{2}$ c. milk

1 Tbl. sugar
1 (3 oz.) pkg. straw-
    berry gelatin
1 c. chopped straw-
    strawberries
1 c. whipping cream,
    whipped

Mix together graham cracker crumbs, sugar and butter. Press mixture into 8 or 9-inch square pan. Chill. Dissolve gelatin in boiling water. Add cold water and chill until thick and consistency of syrup. Add strawberries. Meanwhile, heat marshmallows in milk over medium heat until melted; cool. Fold cooled mixture into whipped cream. Spread half of marshmallow mixture over crumbs. Spoon gelatin mixture on top. Top with remaining marshmallow mixture. Use a spatula to swirl layers to give marbled effect. Chill until set. Makes 9 servings.

* * *

STRAWBERRY KISS

1 (10 oz.) pkg. frozen
    strawberries
2 c. miniature marshmallows

1/3 c. Port wine
1 c. dairy sour cream
Dash of salt

Crush thawed strawberries thoroughly. Combine marshmallows with wine and stir over very low heat until marshmallows are completely melted; cool. Stir in strawberries, sour cream and salt. Turn into refrigerator tray and freeze until barely firm. Spoon into sherbet glasses and serve.

* * *

STRAWBERRIES CHANTILLY

4 egg yolks
1/8 tsp. salt
½ c. evaporated milk
4 c. fresh strawberries

4 Tbls. sugar
½ c. milk
1 Tbl. rum flavoring
Whipping cream, whipped

Beat egg yolks with sugar and salt until light in top of small double boiler. Stir in milk and evaporated milk. Cook, stirring constantly over simmering water, 8 minutes or until mixture thickens and coats a metal spoon. Strain at once into a medium size bowl. Stir in rum flavoring; cool. When ready to serve, spoon washed and hulled straw- berries into sherbet dishes, dividing evenly. Pour sauce around strawberries; serve topped with whipped cream. Makes 4 servings.

* * *

STRAWBERRY YOGURT SURPRISE

1 c. milk
½ c. sugar
1 Tbl. unflavored gelatin
½ tsp. vanilla

3 egg whites
2 Tbls. sugar
1 c. plain yogurt
1 qt. strawberries, sliced

Combine milk, ½ cup sugar and gelatin in a saucepan. Stir over low heat until gelatin and sugar are dissolved; cool. Stir in vanilla and chill until mixture mounds. Beat egg whites until they hold soft peaks. Beat in 2 tablespoons sugar, 1 tablespoon at a time and continue beating until meringue holds stiff peaks. Fold meringue into milk mixture. Fold in yogurt and strawberries. Spoon into individual dessert dishes and chill until set. Garnish with whole strawberries, if desired.

* * *

STRAWBERRIES PARISIENNE

1 (3 oz.) pkg. cream cheese
¼ tsp. pumpkin pie spice
1 c. sour cream

1 Tbl. sugar
2 c. fresh strawberries,
   sliced and sweetened

Beat softened cream cheese until fluffy. Stir in sour cream, sugar and pumpkin pie spice until well blended. Spoon alternate layers of cream cheese mixture and straw- berries into 6 parfait glasses, dividing equally.

* * *

STRAWBERRIES BAVARIAN

2 envelopes unflavored
   gelatin
1/3 c. orange juice
½ c. sugar

1 qt. strawberries, washed and hulled
2 c. whipping cream, whipped

Sprinkle gelatin over orange juice; let stand to soften (about 5 minutes). In small saucepan, heat orange juice and gelatin, simmering gently until gelatin is dissolved; cool. Pureé strawberries; stir in gelatin mixture and sugar; chill, stirring occasionally, until mixture begins to thicken. Fold in whipped cream and spoon into an 8-cup mold. Refrigerate several hours. Unmold and garnish with additional strawberries, if desired.

* * *

STRAWBERRY BLEND 'N' GEL

2 envelopes Knox Un-
   flavored Gelatine
½ c. plus 2/3 c. cold milk
1 c. milk, heated to boiling
2 eggs

1/3 c. sugar
1 (10 oz.) pkg. frozen strawberries, partially thawed (do not drain)
1 c. ice cubes (6 to 8)

In 5-cup blender, sprinkle unflavored gelatine over ½ cup cold milk; let stand 3 to 4 minutes. Add hot milk and process at low speed until gelatine is completely dissolved, about 2 minutes. Add eggs, sugar, 2/3 cup milk, and strawberries; process at high speed until blended. Add ice cubes, one at a time; process at high speed until ice is melted. Pour into dessert dishes or bowl and chill until set. Makes about 8 servings.

Reprinted Courtesy of Knox Gelatine, Inc.

* * *

STRAWBERRY COUPE

1 pint fresh strawberries
¼ c. LEROUX Straw-
   berry Liqueur

Sugar to taste
Whipped cream, as garnish

Sprinkle strawberries with Strawberry Liqueur and chill. Add sugar to taste and serve topped with whipped cream.

Reprinted permission of LEROUX Liqueurs.

* * *

STRAWBERRY-CHOCOLATE MOUSSE

2 sq. semi-sweet chocolate
¼ c. water
2 (3 oz.) pkgs. cream
  cheese, softened
¼ c. milk

1 Tbl. sugar
1 (8 oz.) container
  frozen whipped topping,
  thawed
1 pt. strawberries,
  cleaned and sliced

Heat chocolate and water over low heat, stirring constantly until mixture is smooth. Remove from heat and cool. Beat 1 package cream cheese until smooth. Add milk and sugar and blend well. Fold in 2 cups whipped topping and 1 cup strawberries. Spread evenly in 1½-quart soufflé dish. Beat remaining cream cheese and fold into remaining whipped topping. Spread evenly over strawberry mixture. Chill about 3 hours. Unmold onto plate and garnish with additional whipped topping and remaining strawberries. Yield: 6 to 8 servings.

* * *

SCARLET STRAWBERRY ANGEL

2 (10 oz.) pkgs. frozen
  strawberries, thawed
1 (6 oz.) pkg. cherry gelatin
1 lg. angel food cake

1 lg. jar maraschino
  cherries, drained
Whipped cream

Prepare gelatin according to package directions and chill to consistency of egg whites. Break cake into large chunks (size of a tennis ball) and add to gelatin. Add ½ jar of cherries. Add strawberries and juice. Put into large mold and chill several hours until very firm. Unmold and invert on plate. Frost with whipped cream and garnish with remaining cherries and chill until serving time.

* * *

STRAWBERRY CREAM SQUARE

2 (3 oz.) pkgs. straw-
  berry gelatin
2 c. boiling water
2 (10 oz.) pkgs. frozen
  strawberries

1 can (13½ oz.) crushed
  pineapple
2 lg. ripe bananas,
  diced
1 c. sour cream

Dissolve gelatin in boiling water. Add strawberries and stir occasionally until thawed. Add pineapple and bananas. Pour ½ of this mixture into an 8-inch square pan and chill until firm. Spread evenly with sour cream. Pour remaining berry mixture on top. Chill until firm. Cut into 1-inch squares and top with sour cream dollops.

* * *

STRAWBERRIES JUBILEE

1½ qts. vanilla ice cream
2 (10 oz.) pkgs. frozen
   strawberries, drained

3/4 c. currant jelly
½ c. brandy

Make 8 large ice cream balls and freeze on cookie sheet, about 2 hours before serving. Refrigerate 8 serving dishes. At serving time, place ice cream in dishes and bring to the table. In a chafing dish over direct heat, melt currant jelly, stirring constantly; add drained strawberries and heat slowly until simmering. Pour brandy into center of fruit; do not stir. Let brandy heat, undisturbed; when warm, light carefully with match. Spoon flaming fruits over ice cream.

* * *

FROZEN STRAWBERRY DESSERT

1 (10 oz.) pkg. frozen
   strawberries, thawed
1½ c. confectioners'
   sugar

1 egg white
¼ c. lemon juice
1 c. whipping cream,
   whipped

Blend strawberries, sugar, egg white and lemon juice. Beat vigorously for about 5 minutes. Fold in whipped cream and pour into baking dish 8-inch square. Cover and freeze until firm. Serve topped with whipped cream and a fresh strawberry, if desired.

* * *

FLUFFY STRAWBERRY DESSERT

4 c. miniature marshmallows
½ c. milk
1 c. whipping cream, whipped

1 (10 oz.) pkg. frozen
   strawberries, thawed
and drained

Melt 3 cups marshmallows with milk in saucepan over low heat, stirring constantly until smooth. Chill until slightly thickened; mix until well blended. Fold in whipped cream, strawberries and remaining marshmallows. Spoon into dessert dishes and chill. Yield: 6 servings.

* * *

STRAWBERRIES 'N' CREAM

1 pt. strawberries,
   washed and hulled
$\frac{1}{2}$ c. light corn syrup
$\frac{1}{2}$ c. strawberry jam
1 Tbl. lemon juice

$\frac{1}{4}$ c. water
1 envelope unflavored
   gelatin
1 c. whipping cream,
   whipped

Blend first 4 ingredients in blender until smooth. In small saucepan, heat water and gelatin until dissolved. Combine strawberry mixture and gelatin mixture in a small bowl and chill about 1 hour or until mixture begins to thicken. Fold in half of the whipped cream. Spoon into individual dessert cups, cover and chill 2 hours or until set. Before serving, garnish with remaining whipped cream. 6 servings.

* * *

STRAWBERRY-BANANA DESSERT

1 c. sugar
1 c. water
1 qt. strawberries,
   washed and hulled

2 Tbls. cornstarch
3 bananas, thinly sliced
Juice of 1 lemon
Cream

Mix 1 cup sugar and 1 cup water in a saucepan and bring to a boil. Add the strawberries and cook over low heat until strawberries are soft but still whole. Blend cornstarch with small amount of cold water and stir into strawberry mixture. Simmer, stirring for 3 minutes. Add bananas and lemon juice and pour into a serving dish; cool. Serve with cream. Makes 6 servings.

* * *

DOUBLE STRAWBERRIES ROMANOFF

1 c. whipping cream
2 Tbls. orange-flavored
   liqueur
$\frac{1}{2}$ c. Bama Strawberry
   Preserves

Few drops red food
   coloring, optional
1 qt. fresh strawberries,
   cleaned, hulled and
   chilled

In medium bowl, whip cream and liqueur; fold in preserves and food coloring, if desired. Serve over strawberries. Refrigerate leftovers. Makes 4 to 6 servings.

Reprinted permission of Bama Products.

* * *

CLOUD-TOPPED PARFAIT

1 can frozen orange
  juice, thawed
1½ c. Durkee Flaked Coconut
¼ c. sugar
3 Tbls. confectioners' sugar

1 c. whipped cream
3½ c. sliced bananas
2 c. orange sections
½ c. strawberries,
  sliced

Mix orange juice, flaked coconut, sugar. Add confectioners' sugar to whipped cream and fold into orange-coconut mixture. Alternate orange-coconut mixture and fruit in parfait glass. Garnish top with additional coconut. Makes 8-10 servings.

Reprinted permission of Durkee Famous Foods.

* * *

STRAWBERRY MACAROON

1 pkg. (1lb. 3 oz.) yellow
  cake mix
¼ c. water
1 large egg
¼ c. shortening

3½ oz. pkg. (1 1/3 cups)
  Durkee Flaked Coconut
1 c. heavy cream (OR
  1 pkg. whipped topping)
1 qt. fresh strawberries,
  sliced and sweetened

Combine cake mix, water, egg, shortening, and 1 cup coconut. Mix well (mixture will be very thick) and pat into greased 13x9-inch pan. Bake at 350° for 18 to 20 minutes. Cool. Whip cream (or prepare whipped topping mix) and fold in the strawberries. Spread over the baked coconut mixture. Top with remaining coconut. Serves 12.

Reprinted permission of Durkee Famous Foods.

* * *

STRAWBERRY/BANANA PUDDING

1 c. sugar
2½ c. milk
2 Tbls. margarine
1 (3 oz.) pkg. lady fingers,
  cut in thirds
1 envelope whipped topping mix

¼ c. flour
3 eggs, beaten
1 tsp. vanilla
1 pt. fresh strawberries
3 bananas, sliced
1/3 c. toasted coconut

Combine sugar and flour in a 2-quart saucepan. Slowly stir in milk. Add eggs slowly to mixture; cook over medium heat, stirring until thick but do not boil. Remove from heat; add margarine and vanilla; cool. Layer cooled custard, lady fingers, strawberries and bananas in a 2-quart bowl. Chill well. Prepare whipped topping mix according to package directions. Spread topping on pudding; sprinkle with coconut. Makes 8 servings.

* * *

FRESH STRAWBERRY TRIFLE

12 lady fingers, split
3½ c. sliced fresh
   strawberries
¼ c. cocktail sherry
1 (14 oz.) can Eagle
   Brand Sweetened
   Condensed Milk
   (NOT evaporated milk)

1/3 c. ReaLemon Reconsti-
   tuted Lemon Juice
3 egg whites, stiffly
   beaten*
1 c. (½ pt.) whipping
   cream, whipped
Additional whipped
   cream, optional

Line bottom and sides of 2-quart glass serving bowl with lady fingers. Spoon 1½ cups strawberries over bottom; sprinkle with 2 tablespoons sherry. Set aside. In large bowl, combine Eagle Brand, ReaLemon and 1½ cups strawberries; mix well. Thoroughly fold in egg whites, whipped cream and remaining sherry. Spoon into prepared bowl. Chill 4 hours or until set. Top with remaining strawberries and additional whipped cream, if desired. Refrigerate leftovers.

*Use only Grade A clean, uncracked eggs.

Reprinted permission of Borden Eagle Brand Sweetened Condensed Milk and ReaLemon/ReaLime Products.

* * *

CREAMY RICE PUDDING

(with strawberry topping)

3 c. cooked rice
3 c. milk
½ c. sugar

3 Tbls. butter OR
   margarine
1 tsp. vanilla
Strawberry topping*

Combine rice, milk, sugar and butter. Cook over medium heat until thickened, about 30 minutes, stirring often. Add vanilla. Pour into serving dish and chill. Serve, topped with Strawberry Topping.

STRAWBERRY TOPPING: Spoon ¼ cup strawberry preserves on chilled pudding. Prepare according to package directions 1 (2 oz.) package whipped topping mix. Fold in ½ cup strawberry preserves. Mound on pudding.

* * *

FRUIT GLAZED BAKED CUSTARDS

3 eggs
1 (14 oz.) can Eagle
   Brand Sweetened
   Condensed Milk
   (NOT evaporated milk)
1 c. water

1 tsp. vanilla extract
½ c. red currant jelly
2 Tbls. orange-flavored
   liqueur
1 Tbl. cornstarch
Fresh Strawberries

Preheat oven to 350°. In medium bowl, beat eggs; stir in Eagle Brand, water and vanilla. Pour mixture into six 6-ounce custard cups. Set cups in shallow pan; fill pan with 1 inch hot water. Bake 45 to 50 minutes or until knife inserted in center comes out clean. Cool. In small saucepan, combine jelly, liqueur and cornstarch. Cook and stir until jelly melts and mixture comes to a boil. Cool to room temperature. Remove custard from cups. Top with sauce and strawberries. Refrigerate leftovers.

Reprinted permission of Borden Eagle Brand Sweetened Condensed Milk.

* * *

SHOW-OFF STRAWBERRY BONBONS

1 can Eagle Brand
   Sweetened Condensed Milk
   (NOT evaporated milk)
4 (3½ oz.) cans flaked coconut
1 (6 oz.) pkg. straw-
   berry gelatin
1 c. ground blanched almonds

1 tsp. almond extract
Red food coloring
2 c. sifted confec-
   tioners' sugar
¼ c. heavy cream
Green food coloring

In large bowl, combine sweetened condensed milk, coconut, 1/3 c. gelatin, almonds, extract, and enough red food coloring to tint mixture a strawberry shade. Chill until firm enough to handle. Form small amounts (about ½ tablespoon) into strawberry shapes. Sprinkle remaining gelatin into flat dish; roll each strawberry to coat. Place on waxed-paper-lined baking sheet; refrigerate. To make hull, combine sugar, cream and green food coloring. Using pastry bag with open star tip, pipe small amount atop each strawberry. Cover; refrigerate if storing more than several days. Makes about 2½ pounds or about 60 candies.

TIP: Use these colorful bonbons to decorate birthday cakes and holiday fruit cakes.

Reprinted permission of Borden Eagle Brand Sweetened Condensed Milk.

* * *

FRUIT CUP

¼ c. frozen pink
 lemonade concentrate
1 orange, peeled and diced
1 apple, cored and diced
1 peach, pitted and diced

1 banana, peeled and
 sliced
½ c. each strawberries,
 blueberries, green
 grapes and cherries,
 sliced

Place lemonade concentrate in a large bowl and mix gently
with fruits as they are prepared. Chill.

* * *

FRUIT COMBO WITH DRESSING

1 head lettuce
1 nectarine, cut in wedges
1 peach, cut in wedges

2 plums cut in wedges
½ cantaloupe, cut in wedges
1 c. strawberries, halved

Coarsely shred lettuce and arrange on a serving platter.
Arrange fruits on lettuce and serve with Molasses Dressing.
Makes 4 servings.

MOLASSES DRESSING: Blend 1 tablespoon light molasses
with ½ cup sour cream and ½ cup mayonnaise. Serve with
fruits.

* * *

GOLDEN YOGURT DRESSING

½ c. sugar
1 Tbl. cornstarch
¼ tsp. salt
2/3 c. orange juice
1 tsp. grated orange rind

1/3 c. ReaLemon Recon-
 stituted Lemon Juice
2 eggs, beaten
1 (8 oz.) container
 plain yogurt

In a small saucepan, mix sugar, cornstarch, and salt;
stir in juices and rind. Cook over medium heat, stirring
constantly until thick and clear. Slowly stir about ¼
cup cornstarch mixture into beaten eggs; add to remaining
cornstarch mixture in pan. Cook and stir about 1 minute.
Chill thoroughly. Fold in yogurt. Serve on fresh fruit
or gelatin salads. Refrigerate. Makes 2 cups.

Reprinted permission of ReaLemon/ReaLime Products.

* * *

FRUIT AND ICE CREAM SALAD

1 c. whole strawberries,
   washed and hulled
1 medium cantaloupe,
   peeled and diced
2 lg. bananas, sliced

1 c. small marshmallows
½ c. pecan halves
½ c. strawberry ice
   cream
Salad greens

Mix fruits, marshmallows and pecans lightly. Blend mayonnaise and ice cream and stir lightly into fruit mixture. Serve on salad greens.

* * *

RED AND WHITE SURPRISE

1 (8 oz.) carton sour cream
3 (3 oz.) pkgs. straw-
   berry gelatin
3 c. boiling water

1 (15 oz.) pkg. frozen
   strawberries
1 (19 oz.) can crushed
   pineapple

Thaw strawberries at room temperature. Dissolve gelatin in 3 cups boiling water. Add strawberries and full can of pineapple. Pour half the mixture into a large mold, reserving remaining half at room temperature. Refrigerate until fairly firm. Spread sour cream on top of mixture in mold. Pour remaining mixture on top and chill again until set.

* * *

HONEY FRUIT DRESSING

1 c. mayonnaise OR
   salad dressing
2 Tbls. honey

1/3 c. ReaLemon Recon-
   stituted Lemon Juice
¼ tsp. ground ginger

In small bowl, combine ingredients; beat with fork or wire whip until smooth. Serve over fresh fruit. Refrigerate. Makes 1½ cups.

Reprinted permission of ReaLemon/ReaLime Products.

* * *

PINEAPPLE-STRAWBERRY CUP

Wash and hull fresh strawberries; cut fresh pineapple in chunks and arrange both attractively in individual serving dishes. Sprinkle with Cointreau or top with Honey Fruit Dressing, if desired.

* * *

CARDINAL FRUIT SALAD

1 c. Bama Red Plum Jam
1 Tbl. ReaLemon Recon-
   stituted Lemon Juice
¼ c. Kirsch or other cherry-
   flavored liqueur

6 to 8 c. mixed fresh
   fruit (strawberries,
   blueberries, peaches,
   grapes, melon balls,
   etc.)

In small saucepan, combine jam and ReaLemon; cook and
stir over low heat until jam melts. Stir in Kirsch.
Chill. Toss with fruit; cover and chill 4 hours, stirring
occasionally. Makes 8 servings.

Fresh, colorful, easy and delicious!

Reprinted permission of Bama Products and ReaLemon/ReaLime
Products.

* * *

CREAMY FRUIT SALAD

1 (3 oz.) pkg. cream
   cheese, softened
1 Tbl. syrup from canned
   mandarin oranges
1 can mandarin orange
   sections, drained

1 can (13½ oz.) pineapple
   tidbits, drained
1 c. small marshmallows
1/3 c. strawberries,
   cleaned and
   halved

Beat cream cheese with syrup from mandarin oranges until
creamy. Add oranges, pineapple and marshmallows; combine
gently but thoroughly. Lightly fold in strawberry halves.
Chill; serve on lettuce beds.

* * *

FROZEN FRUIT SALAD

1 (3 oz.) pkg. cream
   cheese, softened
1 Tbl. syrup from canned
   mandarin oranges
¼ c. mayonnaise
1 can mandarin orange
   sections, drained

1 can (13½ oz.) pineapple
   tidbits, drained
1 c. small marshmallows
1/3 c. strawberries,
   cleaned and halved
1 envelope dessert
   topping, prepared

Combine cream cheese, syrup and mayonnaise until creamy.
Add mandarin orange sections, pineapple and marshmallows.
Fold strawberries into prepared topping and then into
fruit mixture. Pour into a 1½-quart mold and freeze overnight. Dip in warm water to unmold.

* * *

STRAWBERRY PRETZEL SALAD

1½ c. crushed pretzels
½ c. sugar
½ c. margarine,
  melted
1 (8 oz.) pkg. cream
  cheese, softened
2 c. boiling water

1 (9 oz.) carton frozen
  whipped topping, thawed
½ c. sugar
2 (3 oz.) pkgs. straw-
  berry gelatin
2 (10 oz.) pkgs. frozen
  strawberries

Combine crushed pretzels, ½ cup sugar and margarine. Pat into 9x13-inch pan. Bake 7 minutes at 350°; cool. Mix cream cheese, whipped topping and remaining ½ cup sugar. Spread over crumb mixture and refrigerate. Dissolve gelatin in 2 cups boiling water; add both packages of frozen strawberries and pour over cream cheese mixture. Refrigerate. Makes a delicious salad or dessert!

Jane Jauman

* * *

STRAWBERRY SOUR CREAM SALAD

2 (3 oz.) pkg. straw-
  berry gelatin
1¼ c. boiling water
2 (10 oz.) pkg. straw-
  berries, thawed

1 (10 oz.) can crushed
  pineapple and juice
2 or 3 large bananas,
  sliced
1 c. dairy sour cream

Dissolve gelatin in boiling water. Add strawberries and pineapple. Chill until partially thickened. Add bananas. Turn half of the gelatin mixture into a 9x13-inch pan; chill until firm. Spread sour cream over chilled gelatin. Spoon rest of gelatin mixture over sour cream. Chill several hours.

* * *

STRAWBERRY YUM MOLD

½ c. mayonnaise
1 (8 oz.) pkg. cream cheese
¼ c. orange juice
1 c. boiling water

1 (3 oz.) pkg. straw-
  berry gelatin
1 (10 oz.) pkg. frozen
  strawberries

Blend mayonnaise and cream cheese. Add orange juice. Dissolve gelatin in water and add ½ cup syrup from strawberries. Stir gelatin into mayonnaise mixture; chill until slightly thickened. Fold in drained strawberries. Pour into 1-quart mold and chill until firm.

* * *

CALIFORNIA FRUIT SALAD ROSÉ

1 envelope Knox Un-
   flavored Gelatine
2 Tbls. sugar
3/4 c. boiling water

$1\frac{1}{4}$ c. rosé wine
1 c. thinly sliced peaches
$\frac{1}{2}$ c. sliced banana
$\frac{1}{2}$ c. strawberries, sliced

In medium bowl, mix unflavored gelatine with sugar; add boiling water and stir until gelatine is completely dissolved. Stir in wine. Chill, stirring occasionally, until mixture is consistency of unbeaten egg whites. Fold in peaches, banana and strawberries. Turn into 4-cup mold or bowl and chill until firm. Makes about 6 servings.

Reprinted courtesy of Knox Gelatine, Inc.

* * *

Oddly, the favorite early summer flower of most Americans, and their favorite early summer fruit, are fairly close relatives, being members of the same plant family. They are, of course, the rose and the strawberry.

Related or not, we love them both: The rose adding beauty and glory to our environment, and the fresh strawberry providing a seasonal lift to our menus!

Reprinted courtesy of Durkee Famous Foods.

* * *

FROSTY STRAWBERRY LIME SOUP

2 c. unsweetened straw-
berries, fresh or frozen,
thawed
½ c. water
1/3 c. ReaLime Recon-
stituted Lime Juice

1/3 c. sugar
1 (8 oz.) container
sour cream OR plain
yogurt
Additional strawberries,
for garnish, optional

In blender container, combine strawberries, water, ReaLime
and sugar; blend until smooth. Pour into medium bowl.
Stir in sour cream; mix well. Chill thoroughly. Garnish
with strawberries, if desired. Refrigerate leftovers.

Serve refreshing Frosty Strawberry Lime Soup as an appe-
tizer or dessert!

Reprinted permission of ReaLemon/ReaLime Products.

* * *

STRAWBERRY SOUP

1 (16 oz.) pkg. frozen
strawberries
1 c. orange juice

1 c. brandy
1 c. sour cream

Thaw berries and blend in blender with orange juice and
brandy. Fold in sour cream. Let stand in refrigerator
at least 4 hours. Serve cold with a dollop of sour cream
and a whole strawberry as a garnish, if desired.

* * *

STRAWBERRY OMELETTE

1 egg
Dash of salt
Dash of pepper
1 Tbl. butter or margarine

1/3 c. fresh straw-
  berries, sliced
Sour cream

Beat egg, salt and pepper until blended. Melt butter
in a small fry pan and add egg mixture. When nearly set,
spoon strawberries into the center. Fold in half and
slip the omelette onto a plate. Top with sour cream.

* * *

STRAWBERRY OMELETTE II

2 eggs
2 Tbls. water
Dash of salt
1 tsp. sugar
2 Tbls. butter

$\frac{1}{4}$ c. fresh strawberries,
  sliced
Confectioners' sugar
3 Tbls. Strawberry
  liqueur

Mix eggs, water, salt and sugar. Melt butter in an 8-
inch omelet pan over medium heat until just hot enough
to sizzle a drop of water. Pour in egg mixture. Tilt
pan to hasten flow of uncooked eggs. When nearly set,
spread fruit on half the omelet; fold in half. Dust omelet
with confectioners' sugar, pour strawberry liqueur over
omelet; carefully ignite, tilting pan so liqueur will
burn out.

* * *

FRUITED PANCAKE BAKE

1 can (17 oz.) apricot halves
Ricotta Pancakes (recipe below)
1 c. sliced strawberries

2 Tbls. butter, melted
2 Tbls. honey
2 Tbls. sliced almonds

Drain apricots, reserving 2 tablespoons syrup. Divide
Ricotta Pancakes onto 4 individual baking dishes. Top
with apricots and strawberries. Combine reserved syrup,
butter, honey and almonds; pour over fruit and pancakes.
Bake in 375° oven 15 minutes. Serve warm.

RICOTTA PANCAKES: In blender, combine 1 cup part skim
milk ricotta cheese, 3 eggs, $\frac{1}{4}$ c. whole wheat flour and
1 tablespoon brown sugar. Blend until smooth. Coat large
skillet or griddle with vegetable cooking spray; heat
over medium heat. Pour batter on skillet using $\frac{1}{4}$ cup
for each pancake. Turn pancakes over when bubbles form
on surface; brown other side.

Reprinted permission of California Apricot Advisory Board.

FRESH 'N' FANCY STRAWBERRY ICE CREAM

1 envelope unflavored gelatin
1 c. cold water
1 can Eagle Brand Sweetened
   Condensed Milk

2 c. (1 pt.) light cream
1 Tbl. vanilla extract
2 c. well-mashed, fresh
   strawberries

In small saucepan, soften gelatin in ¼ cup water; heat and stir until dissolved. Stir in remaining water. Proceed according to desired method.

Electric or hand-turned ice cream freezer method:
Combine softened gelatin and remaining ingredients in ice cream freezer container; proceed according to manufacturer's instructions.

Refrigerator-freezer method:
In large bowl, combine softened gelatin and remaining ingredients; blend well. Turn into 13x9-inch baking pan; freeze to a firm mush (about 1 hour). Break into pieces and turn into chilled, large mixer bowl; beat until smooth. Return to pan. Cover with foil and freeze until firm.

Reprinted permission of Eagle Brand Sweetened Condensed Milk.

* * *

HOMEMADE STRAWBERRY ICE CREAM

½ c. sugar
4 c. light cream
1½ tsp. unflavored gelatin
1 qt. fresh strawberries

3/4 c. sugar
2 Tbls. water
1 egg, slightly beaten
1 tsp. vanilla

Combine ½ cup sugar and 2 cups of the cream. Soften gelatin in water; add to sugar mixture. Stir over low heat until gelatin dissolves. Slowly stir a small amount of hot mixture into egg; return to hot mixture. Cook and stir until mixture thickens slightly, about 1 minute. Chill. Crush strawberries with 3/4 cup sugar and add to chilled mixture. Add remaining ingredients (cream, vanilla and salt). Freeze.

* * *

STRAWBERRIES EXTRAVAGANCE

¼ c. sherry
1 quart straw-
   berries, washed

1 c. vanilla ice
   cream, softened

Remove stems on berries and pour sherry over; refrigerate. Serve marinated strawberries over slightly softened ice cream.

* * *

THICK STRAWBERRY WHIP

1 pt. fresh strawberries,
   cleaned and hulled (reserve
   several for garnish)
¼ c. ReaLemon Reconstituted
   Lemon Juice

1 can Eagle Brand
   Sweetened
   Condensed Milk
2 c. crushed ice

In blender container, combine all ingredients in order listed; blend until smooth. If desired, garnish with reserved strawberries. Makes 1 quart. Refrigerate any leftovers. Mixture stays thick and creamy in the refrigerator.

TIP: 2 cups frozen strawberries, thawed, may be substituted for fresh strawberries; drain syrup if using sweetened strawberries.

Reprinted permission of ReaLemon/ReaLime Products and Borden Eagle Brand Condensed Milk Products.

* * *

STRAWBERRY THICKSHAKE

1 quart fresh
   strawberries

1 quart vanilla
   ice cream, softened

Reserve a few strawberries for garnish and pureé remainder in blender. Add the ice cream and blend until smooth. Spoon into tall glasses, garnish with reserved strawberries and serve with long spoons. Yield: 4 (8 oz.) servings.

* * *

STRAWBERRY MILK SMOOTHEE

1 c. cold water
3/4 c. strawberries
1 Tbl. sugar

1 tsp. lemon juice
1 c. crushed ice

Assemble blender. Put all ingredients into blender container, cover and process at FRAPPE (LIQUEFY) until smooth. Top with grated nutmeg. Yield: 2 cups.

Recipe Courtesy Oster.

* * *

STRAWBERRY FREEZE

1 c. grapefruit juice   2 Tbls. honey
½ c. fresh strawberries   2/3 c. club soda, divided

Combine grapefruit juice, strawberries, and honey and
pureé in blender. Pour over crushed ice in 2 tall glasses.
Add 1/3 cup club soda to each glass. Stir. Garnish with
a fresh strawberry, if desired.

* * *

STRAWBERRY LEMON CUBES

3/4 c. sugar   3 c. water
1 c. ReaLemon Recon-   Whole, clean,
    stituted Lemon Juice   strawberries

In a 1-quart pitcher, dissolve sugar in ReaLemon; add
water. Pour into ice cube trays. Place 1 whole strawberry in each section. Freeze. Use in mixed drinks,
carbonated beverages, lemonade or punch.

Reprinted permission of ReaLemon/ReaLime Products.

* * *

DOUBLE STRAWBERRY SHAKES

2 c. milk   ½ c. Bama   Strawberry
2 c. strawberry ice cream   Preserves

In blender container, combine ingredients; blend until
smooth. Refrigerate leftovers. Makes 2 to 4 servings.

Reprinted permission of Bama Products.

* * *

FRUIT-MILK DRINK

Add leftover strawberries, an over-ripe banana or any
other fruit to milk and whirl in a blender!

* * *

102

BIG PARTY STRAWBERRY PUNCH

3 lg. cans unsweetened
    pineapple juice
3 c. orange juice
1½ c. lemon juice
1/3 c. lime juice
1 c. fresh mint leaves

2 c. sugar
Ice block
2 (28 oz.) bottles ginger ale
1 (28 oz.) bottle soda water
2 c. fresh strawberries,
    cleaned and halved

Combine juices, sugar and mint leaves. Chill for at least 2 hours. Remove mint leaves. Place ice block in punch bowl. Carefully pour ginger ale and soda water in bowl at the edge. Add strawberries and float orange, or lemon and lime slices on top. Yield: about 80 servings.

* * *

BERRY SPECIAL DRINK

1 sm. can frozen pineapple-
    orange juice
½ c. fresh or frozen
    strawberries

1 banana, sliced
½ c. vanilla
    ice cream
2 or 3 ice cubes

Combine juice, strawberries, banana and ice cream in blender and blend until thick and creamy. Add ice cubes and blend a few seconds longer. Pour into 2 (8 oz.) glasses and garnish with whipped cream and a whole strawberry, if desired.

Laura Jauman

* * *

STRAWBERRY LIMEADE

2 (10 oz.) pkgs. frozen straw-
    berries in syrup, thawed
3 c. cold water
1 (8 oz.) bottle ReaLime Recon-
    stituted Lime Juice

½ to 3/4 c. sugar
Ice
Whole strawberries or
    mint leaves for
    garnish, optional

In blender container, blend strawberries well. In pitcher, combine pureéd strawberries, water, ReaLime and sugar; stir until sugar dissolves. Serve over ice. Garnish as desired. Makes about 1 3/4 quarts.

Reprinted permission of ReaLemon/ReaLime Products.

* * *

STRAWBERRY DAIQUIRI

2 (10 oz.) pkgs. frozen
   strawberries in syrup,
   partially thawed
½ c. light rum

¼ c. confectioners' sugar
1/3 c. ReaLime Recon-
   stituted Lime Juice
2 c. ice cubes

In blender container, combine all ingredients except ice; blend well. Gradually add ice, blending until smooth. Garnish as desired. Makes about 1 quart.

Reprinted permission of ReaLemon/ReaLime Products.

* * *

TROPICAL SMOOTHIE

3/4 c. unsweetened pine-
   apple juice, chilled
½ c. fresh or frozen un-
   sweetened strawberries
1 sm. banana, sliced

¼ c. light rum
¼ c. ReaLime Recon-
   stituted Lime Juice
¼ c. sugar
1 c. ice cubes

In blender container, combine all ingredients except ice; blend well. Gradually add ice, blending until smooth. Garnish as desired. Serve immediately. Makes about 2 3/4 cups.

A refreshing medley of tart and sweet fruit flavors!

Reprinted permission of ReaLemon/ReaLime Products.

* * *

CHAMPAGNE STRAWBERRY PUNCH FRUIT BOWL

Iced fruits for punch
4 c. fresh strawberries
½ c. granulated sugar

1 4/5-quart bottle sauterne
1 c. cognac
4 4/5 bottles champagne,
   chilled

A day in advance, freeze washed bunches of grapes, whole fresh pears, kumquats, lemons, tangerines and strawberries on cookie sheets. Use the frozen fruits as ice cubes in the punch; they do not dilute the punch and can be eaten later--these are your iced fruits.

In a large bowl, sprinkle strawberries with sugar. Add sauterne and cognac; refrigerate to blend the flavors together. Just before serving, arrange iced fruits in punch bowl; pour in strawberry mixture; slowly add champagne. Makes 36 ½-cup servings.

* * *

STRAWBERRIES & FLUFF TOPPING
(for waffles)

2 c. washed and hulled   1 c. whipping cream
   strawberries   1 c. vanilla
2 Tbls. sugar   ice cream

Mash strawberries coarsely. Stir in sugar. Pour over
waffles. Whip cream until stiff, but will not hold shape.
Add the ice cream by the spoonful beating just until
smooth. Spoon on top of waffle and sauce.

* * *

STRAWBERRY GLAZE
(for turkey)

1 (10 oz.) pkg. frozen   1 Tbl. cornstarch
   strawberries   1/8 tsp. ground cloves
2 Tbls. lemon juice   Pinch of salt

Drain strawberries, placing juice in a measuring cup.
Add lemon juice and fill with water to 3/4 cup measure.
Pour juice into saucepan. In a small bowl, mix cornstarch,
cloves, and salt with a small amount of juice. Add to
saucepan and cook and stir until thickened. Stir in strawberries and let cool slightly. Spoon over roast turkey
when it is removed from the oven. Serve remaining glaze
with sliced turkey.

Reprinted permission of Swift & Company.

* * *

STRAWBERRY & BRANDY PRESERVES

1 (8 oz.) jar   1½ oz. brandy
   strawberry preserves

Blend together in a bowl and return to jar. Store in
refrigerator.

* * *

STRAWBERRY WHEAT GERM BOUNCE

1 pkg. (10 oz.) frozen strawberries, partially thawed
1 carton (8 oz.) plain yogurt
½ c. unsweetened
   pineapple juice

¼ c. Kretschmer Wheat
   Germ, Regular or Brown
   Sugar & Honey
2 Tbls. honey,
   optional

Assemble KITCHEN CENTER "Osterizer" blender. Put all ingredients in blender container. Cover and blend at LIQUEFY about 1 minute. Makes 2 3/4 cups.

Recipe Courtesy Oster.

* * *

STRAWBERRY COOLER

4 Tbls. lemonade concen-
   trate, thawed, undiluted
3/4 c. water

1 c. strawberries
1½ c. crushed ice

Assemble Blender. Put all ingredients into blender container, cover and process at FRAPPE (LIQUEFY) until slushy. Yield: 3 cups.

Recipe Courtesy Oster.

* * *

BERRYBERRY ORANGE JUICE

3 c. fresh strawberries
3 c. orange juice

3 Tbls. sugar
1/3 c. Leroux Truskawkowy
   Strawberry Liqueur

Combine all ingredients and place half of mixture at a time in blender; serve over crushed ice with a straw.

Recipe courtesy Leroux Liqueurs.

* * *

STRAWBERRY BOUNCE

1 quart fresh strawberries,
   thoroughly washed

1 to 2 c. sugar
Fifth vodka or bourbon

Add to a sterilized clear glass half-gallon bottle, the strawberries, 1 cup sugar and the vodka or bourbon. Seal and shake vigorously at least once a day. Follow this "bouncing" procedure for approximately one month and filter to remove berry mash. Additional sugar can be added during the "bouncing" time, if deisred. Filter slowly through a clean cloth, as often as necessary to obtain best clarity.

* * *

STRAWBERRY-RHUBARB JAM

(Good Old-Fashioned Flavor)

2 thick stalks rhubarb,
   about 18 inches long
1 quart strawberries,
   hulled and washed
2 Tbls. lemon juice

$\frac{1}{4}$ tsp. salt
1 pkg. (1 3/4 oz.)
   powdered fruit pectin
$5\frac{1}{2}$ c. sugar

Assemble Food Grinder with Coarse Disc. Grind rhubarb and strawberries. Add lemon juice, salt and pectin. Cook and stir until boiling. Add sugar. Stirring constantly, boil 1 minute. Turn off heat source. Stir and skim 5 minutes. Ladle into hot canning jars, leaving $\frac{1}{2}$-inch headspace. Seal and process in a simmering water bath 10 minutes. Yield: 6 pints.

Recipe Courtesy Oster.

* * *

STRAWBERRY PINEAPPLE JAM

2 c. prepared strawberries
$\frac{1}{2}$ c. undrained crushed
   pineapple
$4\frac{1}{2}$ c. sugar

$\frac{1}{4}$ c. lemon juice
1 pouch liquid
   fruit pectin

Stem and thoroughly crush, one layer at a time, about 1 quart strawberries. Measure 2 cups into large bowl or pan. Add pineapple. Thoroughly mix sugar into fruit; let stand 10 minutes. Add lemon juice to fruit pectin in small bowl. Stir into fruit; stir continuously for 3 minutes. (A few sugar crystals will remain). Ladle quickly into scalded containers. Cover at once with tight lids. Let stand at room temperature 24 hours; then store in freezer. Small amounts may be covered and stored in refrigerator up to 3 weeks. Makes about $5\frac{1}{2}$ cups or about 6 containers of jam.

* * *

EASY STRAWBERRY JAM

2 (10 oz.) pkgs. frozen
   strawberries, thawed
$2\frac{1}{2}$ c. sugar

$\frac{1}{4}$ of a 6 oz. bottle
   fruit pectin
Melted paraffin

Combine thawed strawberries and sugar in heavy 4-quart saucepan and mix well. Bring to a boil over high heat and boil rapidly 1 minute, stirring constantly. Remove from heat and immediately stir in fruit pectin. Skim off foam with metal spoon, then stir and skim 5 minutes to cool slightly and prevent fruit from floating. Ladle into sterilized jars and seal at once with 1/8-inch paraffin. Cool completely. Makes about 3 cups.

STRAWBERRY BUTTER

2 c. prepared fruit	4 c. sugar
½ tsp. grated lemon rind	2 Tbls. lemon juice
¼ tsp. nutmeg	1 pouch liquid fruit pectin

Stem about 1 quart strawberries and place a few pieces
at a time in blender container so blades are just covered.
Cover container; chop fruit (do not pureé). Measure 2
cups into large bowl or pan. Add lemon rind and nutmeg.
Thoroughly mix sugar into fruit; let stand 10 minutes.
Add lemon juice to fruit pectin in a small bowl. Stir
into fruit. Continue stirring 3 minutes. (A few sugar
crystals will remain). Quickly ladle into scalded containers. Cover at once with tight lids. Let stand at
room temperature 24 hours; then store in freezer. Small
amounts may be covered and stored in refrigerator up to
3 weeks. Makes about 4 cups.

* * *

STRAWBERRY-PINEAPPLE PRESERVES

1 (10 oz.) pkg. frozen strawberries	2 Tbls. lemon juice
2 c. crushed pineapple	5 c. sugar
	1 c. liquid pectin

Heat together strawberries, pineapple, and lemon juice
and sugar. Bring to a boil and stir 1 minute. Remove
from heat; mix in liquid pectin. Skim and stir 5 minutes.
Pour into 12 sterilized (4 oz.) jars and seal.

* * *

STRAWBERRY JAM VERMOUTH

2 c. prepared strawberries	3/4 c. water
¼ c. dry white vermouth	1 box (1 3/4 oz.) pow-
4 c. sugar	dered fruit pectin

Stem and thoroughly crush, one layer at a time, about
1 quart strawberries. Measure 2 cups into large bowl
or pan. Add vermouth. Thoroughly mix sugar into fruit;
let stand 10 minutes. Mix water and fruit pectin in small
saucepan. Bring to a full boil and boil 1 minute, stirring
constantly. Stir into fruit. Continue stirring 3 minutes.
(A few sugar crystals will remain). Ladle quickly into
scalded containers. Cover at once with tight lids. Let
stand at room temperature 24 hours; then store in freezer.
Small amounts may be covered and stored in refrigerator
up to 3 weeks. Makes about 3 3/4 cups or about 6 (8 oz.)
containers.

* * *

SWEET STRAWBERRY BUTTER

1 pkg. (10 oz.) frozen   1 c. butter OR
   strawberries, thawed   margarine, softened
1 c. confectioners' sugar

In blender container, combine all ingredients, cover and
blend on high speed until completely smooth. Delicious
served on hot muffins! Makes 2½ cups.

* * *

STRAWBERRY LEMON DRESSING

2/3 c. strawberry jelly   ½ tsp. celery salt
1 c. salad oil   ¼ tsp. salt
½ c. lemon juice   Dash of cayenne
2 tsp. dry mustard

Put all ingredients in blender and whirl at high speed
until smooth. Serve on fruit salad or greens. Makes
about 2 cups.

* * *

STRAWBERRIES ALA STRAWBERRIES

1½ quarts fresh strawberries, 1 Tbl. sugar
   washed and hulled   1 Tbl. kirsch
1/3 c. strawberry jelly

Place 1 quart of prepared strawberries in serving dish
and chill. Place remaining strawberries in blender container and combine with sugar, jelly (not preserves) and
kirsch. Blend for a few seconds. Pour into a separate
serving dish and chill. Accompany berries with sauce.

* * *

STRAWBERRY TREASURE SUNDAES

2 c. vanilla ice cream   ¼ c. flaked coconut
½ c. strawberry jam

Soften ice cream slightly. Alternate layers of ice cream
and jam in four 9-ounce paper cold drink cups. Top with
a spoonful of strawberry jam and sprinkle a ring of coconut
around jam. Freeze at least 4 hours or until firm.

* * *

BILBERRIES
BLACKBERRIES
CURRANTS
ELDERBERRIES
GOOSEBERRIES
MULBERRIES
THIMBLEBERRIES

MISCELLANEOUS BERRIES

FREEZING BERRIES

BILBERRIES, BLUEBERRIES AND ELDERBERRIES can be frozen just as they come from the bush. When your recipe calls for the berry you need, simply remove the desired amount from the freezer, rinse, drain and proceed with your recipe.

CRANBERRIES should be firm, deep-red berries with glossy skins. Stem and sort. Wash and drain. Pack into containers without sugar. Leave head space, seal and freeze.

CURRANTS should be plump, fully ripe and bright red. Wash in cold water and remove stems. Pack, unsweetened, into containers, leaving head space; seal and freeze.

GOOSEBERRIES may be frozen with syrup or without sweetening. For use in pie or preserves, the unsweetened pack is better. Choose fully ripe berries if freezing for pie--berries a little underripe for jelly making. Sort, remove stems and blossom ends, and wash. Pack into containers without sugar. Leave head space, seal and freeze.

RASPBERRIES may be frozen in sugar or syrup or unsweetened. Select fully ripe, juicy berries. Sort, wash carefully in cold water, and drain thoroughly.
SUGAR PACK: To 1 quart raspberries, add 3/4 cup sugar and mix carefully to avoid crushing. Put into containers, leaving head space; seal and freeze.
UNSWEETENED PACK: Put berries into containers, leave head space, seal and freeze.

STRAWBERRIES should be firm, ripe red berries preferably with a slightly tart flavor. Large berries are better sliced or crushed. Sort berries, wash in cold water, drain well and remove hulls. Sugar and syrup packs make better quality frozen strawberries than berries packed without sweetening.
SUGAR PACK: Same as for raspberries.
UNSWEETENED PACK: Pack into containers, leaving head space. For better color, cover with water containing 1 teaspoon crystalline ascorbic acid to each quart of water. Seal; freeze.

SYRUP PACK: All of the above berries can be packed in a 50% type syrup which consists of 4 3/4 cups sugar, 4 cups water, which yields $6\frac{1}{2}$ cups syrup. Dissolve sugar in cold or hot water. If hot water is used, cool syrup before using. Syrup may be made up the day before and kept cold in the refrigerator. When packing fruit into containers, be sure the syrup covers the fruit, so that the top pieces will not change in color and flavor. To keep fruit under the syrup, place a small piece of crumpled waxed paper on top and press fruit down into syrup before closing and sealing the container.

BILBERRY TEA CAKE

2 Tbls. butter or margarine   1/3 c. water
1 c. sugar   1 egg, separated
1½ c. cake flour   1½ c. bilberries

Cream butter and sugar. Add egg yolk. Stir flour and
water alternately into creamed mixture. Fold in stiffly
beaten egg white. Pour ½ batter into greased 8-inch pan,
top with berries. Add remaining batter. Bake 350° for
35 minutes. Sprinkle with confectioners' sugar while
still hot.

* * *

BILBERRY BOUNCE

1 quart bilberries,   2 c. sugar
   washed and drained   Fifth vodka or bourbon

Use a half-gallon clear glass bottle, sterilized, and
add to the bottle the berries, sugar and vodka or bourbon.
Seal and shake vigorously at least once a day. Follow
this "bouncing" procedure for approximately one month
and filter to remove berry mash. To obtain the best clarity, several slow filterings through a clean cloth or
coffee filters is recommended. If cloudiness occurs at
a future date, filter again.

NOTE: Wild raspberries are also delicious when used to
make "bounce." Chokecherries can also be used and will
produce an "almond nutty" flavor to your bounce.

* * *

BILBERRY FLUMMERY

2½ c. bilberries   ½ c. sugar
1½ c. water   Grated rind and juice
2 Tbls. cornstarch   of 1 lemon

Wash and drain bilberries. Combine cornstarch and sugar.
Stir in remaining ingredients. Cook over low heat, stirring constantly until mixture bubbles and thickens. Spoon
into individual serving dishes and chill. Garnish with
whipped cream, if desired, before serving. Makes 4
servings.

* * *

BLACKBERRY FLUMMERY

2 c. blackberries
¼ c. cornstarch
½ to 3/4 c. sugar

Dash of salt
Juice of ½ lemon
Sour or sweet cream

Wash and drain blackberries, then put in a saucepan with 1 cup water and simmer about 5 minutes. Force through a sieve. Add enough water to make 2½ cups puree. Mix cornstarch, sugar and salt and add to berry puree. Cook, stirring until clear and thickened. Add lemon juice and cool, stirring occasionally. Chill and serve with either sour cream or sweet cream. If you prefer not to sieve the blackberries, reduce cornstarch to 3 tablespoons. Makes 4 servings.

* * *

BLACKBERRY SUNDAE SURPRISE

1 lg. box black
  raspberry gelatin
1 quart vanilla ice cream

1 (2½ lb.) can fruit
  cocktail, drained
1½ c. blackberries

Wash and drain blackberries. Dissolve gelatin in 2 cups boiling water. Scoop ice cream into 8 tall sherbet glasses. Gently fold blackberries into fruit cocktail and add 2 spoonfuls of fruit mixture to the ice cream. Pour warm gleatin over top. Serve at once. The sauce will gel as you eat it.

* * *

WILD BLACKBERRY SUNDAE TOPPING

1 quart wild blackberries

1 c. sugar

Wash and drain berries. Cook blackberries for 5 minutes, mashing while cooking. Add sugar and cook until slightly thickened. Ladle into hot jars. Adjust lids at once and process in boiling water bath for 5 minutes. Remove from canner and complete seals. Delicious ice cream sauce!

* * *

BLACKBERRY BLEND

1 c. fresh blackberries
1 c. plain yogurt

1 c. skim milk
2 Tbls. honey

Whirl all ingredients in blender until berries are pureed. If desired, pour through strainer to remove seeds. Makes 3 cups.

* * *

BLACKBERRY OAT BARS

3/4 c. butter OR
   margarinc, softened
1 c. firmly packed light
   brown sugar
2 tsp. grated
   lemon rind

$1\frac{1}{2}$ c. unsifted flour
1 tsp. salt
$\frac{1}{2}$ tsp. baking soda
$1\frac{1}{2}$ c. rolled oats
1 c. Bama Blackberry
   Preserves

Preheat oven to 400° (375°) for glass dish). In large mixer bowl, cream butter, sugar, and rind. Stir together dry ingredients; add to butter mixture. Mix well. Press half of oat mixture into well-greased 13x9-inch baking pan. Spread preserves over oat mixture. Crumble remaining oat mixture over top; press down lightly. Bake 20 to 25 minutes or until lightly browned. Cool. Cut into bars. Makes 2 dozen bars.

Reprinted permission of Bama Products.

* * *

CRUSTLESS BLACKBERRY TOPPED CHEESE PIE

2 (8 oz.) pkg. cream
   cheese, softened
1 c. sugar
4 eggs
2 tsp. lemon OR
   vanilla extract

1 tsp. grated lemon
   rind, optional
1 c. sour cream (8 oz.)
1 (16 oz.) jar Bama
   Blackberry Preserves,
   chilled

Preheat oven to 350°. In large mixer bowl, beat cream cheese and sugar until fluffy. Add eggs, one at a time, beating well after each addition. Stir in 1 teaspoon extract and, if desired, rind. Pour into well-buttered 9-inch pie plate. Bake 25 to 30 minutes or until lightly browned around edges. Remove from oven; let stand 10 minutes.

Meanwhile, stir together sour cream and remaining extract. Spread evenly over pie; bake 10 minutes longer. Cool slightly. Top with preserves. Chill thoroughly. Refrigerate leftovers.

Reprinted permission of Bama Products.

* * *

SOUTHERN JAM CAKE

1 c. butter OR
   margarine, softened
1 c. sugar
5 eggs
1 (16 oz.) jar Bama
   Blackberry Jam
1 c. Bama Strawberry Preserves
3 c. unsifted flour

1 Tbl. baking soda
2 tsp. ground allspice
2 tsp. ground cinnamon
½ tsp. ground cloves
1 c. buttermilk
Maple Frosting*
Chopped nuts,
   optional

Preheat oven to 350°. In large mixer bowl, cream butter and sugar. Add eggs, one at a time, beating well after each addition. Stir in jam and preserves. Sift or stir together dry ingredients; add alternately to jam mixture with buttermilk. Mix well. Turn into 3 well-greased, wax-paper-lined 9-inch layer cake pans. Bake 40 minutes or until toothpick inserted near center comes out clean. Cool 5 minutes; remove from pans. Cool completely. Frost with Maple Frosting and if desired, garnish with nuts.

*MAPLE FROSTING: In large mixer bowl, beat 1 (8 oz.) package softened cream cheese until fluffy. Add 1½ pounds (about 6 cups) confectioners' sugar, sifted, 2 teaspoons maple flavoring, a dash of salt and 1 to 2 tablespoons milk. Mix well. Add additional milk, 1 teaspoon at a time, for desired consistency.

Reprinted permission of Bama Products.

* * *

CHOCOLATE JAM CUPCAKES

1 (9 oz.) pkg. (one-layer)
   devil's food cake mix
½ c. water
1 egg

½ c. Bama Blackberry
   Jam
¼ c. chopped nuts
White or chocolate
   frosting, optional

Preheat oven to 350°. In mixer bowl, combine cake mix, water and egg; beat according to package directions. Stir in jam and nuts. Spoon into paper-lined muffin cups. Bake 15 to 20 minutes or until toothpick inserted in center comes out clean. Cool. Frost, if desired. Makes about 1½ dozen cupcakes.

Reprinted permission of Bama Products.

* * *

WILD BLACKBERRY JAM

5 lbs. wild ripe
  blackberries
6 c. sugar

Grated rind of
  one lemon
Juice of 2 lemons
½ c. water

Place washed and drained blackberries on paper towels to dry. In a pot, combine sugar and water and bring to a boil. Lower heat and boil gently for 2 or 3 minutes. Pour berries into boiling syrup, stirring them well and letting them come to a boil. Set pot aside for 4 hours. Stir in lemon rind. Bring to a boil and stir; skim off foam. Boil slowly until thick. Stir in lemon juice and reheat to boiling. Pour while hot into sterilized jars. Seal and store in a cool, dark, dry place.

* * *

BLACKBERRY PUDDING WITH LEMON SAUCE

½ c. flour
½ tsp. salt
1 tsp. baking soda

2 eggs, beaten
2 c. milk
2 c. blackberries

Sift dry ingredients together, add eggs and mix in milk. Dredge berries in flour and fold into pudding mix. Bake at 350° in greased 9x13-inch baking pan for 1½ hours. Serve with Lemon Sauce.*

NOTE: Blueberries or raspberries can also be used.

*LEMON SAUCE: Make a syrup by boiling 3/4 cup sugar and ¼ cup water for 5 minutes. Remove from stove and add 2 tablespoons butter and 1 tablespoon lemon juice. Cook until thickened. Makes about 1 cup.

* * *

CURRANTS AND APPLES IN BARBECUE SAUCE

2 c. canned apple
   slices, undrained
½ c. chili sauce
1 Tbl. cider vinegar
¼ c. brown sugar

½ c. currants
Dash of salt
2½ tsp. Worcester-
   shire Sauce
2 tsp. dry mustard

Combine all ingredients, bring to a boil and simmer, covered, for about 15 minutes. Serve as a relish with meats
or baked beans. Makes about 3 cups.

* * *

GLAZED HAMS WITH GRENADINE PEARS

Fully Cooked Swift Premium
   Hostess Hams
2 jars (8 oz. ea.) red
   currant jelly

¼ c. grenadine syrup
2 tsp. lemon juice
¼ tsp. ground
   ginger

Place hams on a rack in a shallow open pan. Do not add
water. Do not cover. Insert a roast meat thermometer
into the meatiest part of each ham. Heat in a slow oven
(325°) to an internal temperature of 140°F., about 1¼
to 1½ hours for half ham or 1 3/4 to 2 hours for whole
ham.

In top of a double boiler, combine currant jelly and remaining ingredients. Heat until smooth in consistency.
During the last 15 minutes of the heating time, remove
hams and top with all but ¼ cup of currant glaze. Return
to oven and complete heating. Serve garnished with Grenadine Pears.

GRENADINE PEARS: Pare skin from 12 small whole pears,
keeping stems intact. Slice approximately ¼ inch off
bottom of pears so they will stand upright. Brush each
pear with lemon juice and sprinkle with granulated sugar.
Place in baking dish. Combine 3/4 cup water and 2 tablespoons grenadine and pour into bottom of dish. Cover.
Bake in a slow oven (325°F.), basting occasionally, until
tender and slightly pink in color, approximately 45 minutes
to 1 hour. During the last 10 minutes boil ½ cup sugar,
½ cup water and 2 tablespoons grenadine in a saucepan
until a heavy syrup forms. Glaze pears with this syrup
mixture. If desired, dribble 1 teaspoon of ham glaze
on top of each pear. Serve as a garnish around ham on
the platter.

Reprinted permission of Swift & Company.

CURRANT DROP COOKIES

1 c. butter OR
   margarine, softened
1 c. sugar
1 egg, slightly beaten
1 tsp. vanilla

1 tsp. grated lemon rind
1 c. currants, scalded
   and drained
2 1/3 c. sifted all-
   purpose flour

Cream butter and sugar together until fluffy. Add remaining ingredients and mix well. Drop by teaspoonfuls 2 inches apart of greased cookie sheet and bake at 375° for 10 minutes or until lightly brown around the edges. Remove at once. Makes about 7 dozen cookies.

* * *

GRANDMOTHER'S SPICIE COOKIES

4 c. flour
1½ tsp. baking soda
1½ tsp. cinnamon
½ tsp. nutmeg
¼ tsp. cloves
1½ c. sugar

1 c. butter OR
   margarine, softened
2 eggs
1 Tbl. milk
1 c. dried
   currants

Beat butter and sugar until fluffy; beat in eggs until well blended. Combine dry ingredients. Beat in milk and then add dry ingredients. Stir in currants. Refrigerate dough until cold. Roll dough on floured board as thin as possible and cut into shapes. Bake on cookie sheet 8 to 10 minutes or until lightly brown (375° oven). Makes about 100 cookies, depending on size of shapes.

* * *

CURRANT COOKIES

1 c. sugar, heaped
4 c. flour
4 tsp. baking powder
1 tsp. salt
Dash of nutmeg

1 c. shortening OR
   margarine
1 tsp. lemon extract
1 egg
3/4 c. milk*
1 c. currants

Combine all dry ingredients. Cut in shortening. Add currants. Then add liquid. Dough should be a little sticky. If too dry, add a little more milk. Roll on floured board. Sprinkle with sugar. Cut thick. Bake 425° for 10 to 12 minutes. Handle dough as little as possible.

*NOTE: Sour milk or buttermilk may be used; however, use only 1 teaspoon baking soda and 1 teaspoon baking powder.

* * *

BAMA COOKIE GEMS

½ c. shortening
3/4 c. sugar
1 egg
1 tsp. vanilla extract
2 2/3 c. unsifted flour
½ tsp. salt

¼ tsp. baking powder
¼ tsp. baking soda
½ c. sour cream
1¼ c. finely chopped nuts
Bama Currant Jelly OR any
    flavor Bama Jams,
    Jellies or Preserves

Preheat oven to 400°. In large mixer bowl, combine shortening, sugar, egg and vanilla; mix well. Sift or stir
together dry ingredients. Add to shortening mixture alternately with sour cream; mix well. Shape into 1¼-inch
balls; roll in nuts. Place 1 inch apart on greased baking
sheets. Press thumb in center of each ball; fill with
jelly. Bake 10 to 12 minutes or until lightly browned.
Makes about 4½ dozen gems.

TIP: Bama Cookie Gems can be made ahead and frozen.

Reprinted permission of Bama Products.

* * *

CURRANT PUDDING WITH HARD SAUCE

2 3/4 c. beef suet,
    ground, (½ pound)
2 c. fine dry bread crumbs
1 c. flour
1 c. sugar
1 c. finely chopped
    blanched almonds
1 c. currants
2/3 c. light raisins
½ c. brandy or rum
1½ tsp. grated lemon peel

2/3 c. mixed candied
    fruits and peels
½ c. dark raisins
½ tsp. nutmeg
½ tsp. cinnamon
½ tsp. allspice
½ tsp. salt
3/4 c. milk
4 eggs,
    slightly beaten
¼ c. lemon juice

In a large bowl, combine suet, crumbs, flour, sugar, almonds, fruits, spices, and salt; mix well. Combine remaining ingredients; stir into fruit mixture and mix
thoroughly. Turn into well-greased 7½ cup ovenproof bowl
or mold; cover tightly. Place on rack in deep kettle
or dutch oven. Pour boiling water in kettle to 1 inch
depth; cover kettle. Gently boil water, steaming pudding
5 hours. Cool about 30 minutes. Unmold. Cool completely.
Wrap in foil; store in refrigerator until ready to use.
To reheat, steam foil-wrapped pudding using steaming method
above for 1 to 1½ hours. Serve with Hard Sauce.*

*HARD SAUCE: Thoroughly cream together 1 cup butter or
margarine and 4 cups confectioners' sugar. Stir in 2
teaspoons vanilla. Beat until fluffy.

* * *

119

ELDERBERRY PIE

2½ c. elderberries,
  washed and drained
1 c. crab apples,
  peeled and chopped
1 c. sugar
¼ tsp. salt

¼ c. flour
1½ Tbls. butter OR
  margarine
1 Tbl. lemon juice
Pastry for 2 crust
  9-inch pie

Sprinkle elderberries with lemon juice. Crush 1 cup of the berries and combine with crab apples, sugar, salt and flour, mixing well. Gently fold in remaining berries and spoon into pastry-lined pie pan. Dot with butter and apply top crust. Cut slits in top crust to allow steam to escape. Bake 30 to 40 minutes at 400° or until filling bubbles, apples are tender and crust is nicely brown.

* * *

MULBERRY PIE

Pastry for 2 crust
  9-inch pie
2 c. mulberries,
  washed and
  drained

1 c. rhubarb,
  finely chopped
3/4 c. sugar
2 Tbls. cornstarch
1½ Tbls. butter

Combine mulberries and rhubarb in a bowl. Gently mix in sugar and cornstarch. Turn mixture into pastry-lined pan. Dot with butter and top with second crust. Cut slits in top crust to allow steam to escape. Bake 45 to 50 minutes at 425° or until filling bubbles and crust is nicely brown.

* * *

GOOSEBERRY PIE I

3 c. gooseberries,
  washed and drained
1½ c. sugar
3 Tbls. minute
  tapioca

Dash of salt
1½ Tbls. butter OR
  margarine
Pastry for 2 crust
  9-inch pie

Crush 1 cup berries and add sugar, tapioca and salt.
Cook, stirring constantly, until mixture boils; cook 2
minutes. Remove from heat and add remaining berries.
Pour into pastry-lined pie plate and dot with butter.
Apply top crust, cutting slits to allow steam to escape.
Bake at 400° for 30-35 minutes or until done.

* * *

GOOSEBERRY PIE II

3 c. gooseberries,
  washed and drained
½ c. water
¼ tsp. salt
½ tsp. cloves

1 Tbl. butter
1½ c. sugar
2 Tbls. flour
1 tsp. cinnamon
1/8 tsp. nutmeg

Combine gooseberries, sugar and water and cook until berries are tender, about 5 or 6 minutes. Sift remaining
dry ingredients together and stir in the cooked mixture
and let cool. While gooseberry mixture is cooling, prepare
pastry for a 2 crust 9-inch pie plate. Pour berry mixture
into pie shell and dot with butter. Cover with top crust
and slash to allow steam to escape. Bake at 450° for
10 minutes, then reduce to 350° and continue baking for
25 minutes longer.

* * *

GOOSEBERRY FOOL

1 quart gooseberries
1 c. sugar

3/4 c. water
1½ c. whipping cream,
  whipped

Remove stems, wash and drain gooseberries. Combine all
ingredients except whipping cream and cook over low heat
until tender. Cook, stirring often, until sauce is thickened. Put berries through a food mill or fine sieve and
chill. Just before serving, fold gooseberry sauce into
whipped cream. Serve immediately.

* * *

When ripe, thimbleberries are bright red and easily picked. They frequently are used in jam, but experimenting with thimbleberries in recipes that use raspberries can yield some interesting results!

THIMBLEBERRY JAM

2 c. thimbleberries   2 c. sugar

Pick over berries, wash and drain. Mash with sugar and heat to boiling. Boil 3 to 5 minutes. Fill sterilized jars and seal.

* * *

THIMBLEBERRY FREEZER JAM

1 qt. fresh thimbleberries   3/4 c. water
1 to 2 c. sugar   1 pkg. powdered pectin

Wash and drain thimbleberries, discarding those that are too dry. Measure and crush one layer of berries at a time in a mixing bowl. Add sugar and mix thoroughly. Additional sugar may be added, if desired. Let stand for 10 minutes for juicing to begin. In a small saucepan, blend water and powdered pectin. Cook over low heat, stirring constantly to prevent sticking, until mixture boils. Boil hard for 1 minute. Add syrup to fruit, blending well. Continue stirring for two minutes. Ladle jam into clean, sterilized containers and cover at once. Let stand at room temperature for 24 hours. Store in refrigerator if to be used within 3 weeks. Store remainder jam in freezer.

* * *

THIMBLEBERRY PUDDING

1 qt. fresh thimbleberries   3 Tbls. cornstarch
½ c. sugar   ½ c. water

Hull, rinse and pat thimbleberries dry with paper towel. Puree in an electric blender or rub berries through a sieve. Combine berries and remaining ingredients in a medium saucepan and bring to a boil, stirring constantly; reduce heat and simmer until thickened. Chill. Before serving, top with whipped cream, if desired.

* * *